D0378649

Role Playing
in Leadership Training
and Group Problem Solving

ROLE PLAYING IN LEADERSHIP TRAINING AND GROUP PROBLEM SOLVING

By *ALAN F. KLEIN*

ASSOCIATION PRESS
NEW YORK

ROLE PLAYING
IN LEADERSHIP TRAINING
AND GROUP PROBLEM SOLVING

Association Press, 291 Broadway, New York 7, N.Y.

Library of Congress catalog card number: 56-6449

55

Printed in the United States of America
American Book–Stratford Press, Inc., New York

To

Opal Boynton

Introduction

This book is about training ourselves in more effective methods for improving our organizational life. It is specifically about a method called role playing, through which we may achieve more widespread and vital participation at meetings. It is about helping members to gain skill as members and as leaders, and thereby to solve their group problems more efficiently.

It is said that we Americans are joiners. Every community is organized with hundreds of clubs and other groups to which people belong. Many of these organizations are seeking answers to operational problems. How shall they find and train leaders, deal with domineering chairmen, cut-and-dried agenda, self-perpetuating cliques? How shall they cope with apathy and indifference, poor attendance, unwillingness to take office, lack of communication? What methods shall they use to solve their problems and to train themselves to meet the demands of complicated group life?

If we are to achieve a more efficient and more satisfying organizational operation we must train for leadership and train in human relations. For too long we have trained leaders, the few who run the show. If we are to have a truly democratic and effective society we shall train the leadership potential in all the members, and not the select few. Leadership is but one function of membership. If we are to work in groups, toward common goals, we must prepare ourselves in how to work effectively with other people. This is human relations training. It includes ways of solving our problems together, better participation in organizational efforts, better meetings, and effective shared leadership. The practical way of combating apathy and domination is for people to acquire skills of group participation and thereby to gain a sense of competence and mastery of their destinies.

This book is the result of some years of cumulative experiences in helping groups to improve their methods of group problem solving. Group problem solving as used here means the making of group decisions. It enters into every phase of organizational life, for every time a group does anything, it must make many decisions from the planning to the executing stages. Organizational problems of constitution or structure, membership and officer selection, program planning and its fulfillment, and others, all require solving of problems by the members as a group. Two of the major determining factors that exist within the problem-solving area are human relations and leadership. To improve problem solving requires the improvement of the human relations and leadership skills of the members.

The author's experience as a training adviser to community groups of all kinds has demonstrated that role playing is a useful and appropriate method for training in group problem solving and leadership. It is presented here as one way to help you to achieve your organizational goals more readily.

The book is designed to take the group member through role playing from beginning to end, with detailed instructions for doing at every step. Each section contains the principles applicable to the phase of the subject being discussed, with illustrations and examples of how it was done. The illustrative material has been tested in practice and is offered to clarify the principles and to be used as a model for the reader to adapt to his own particular organizational use.

The first chapters endeavor to show how role

playing is developed and how it can be used. There is an explanation of how, in role playing, roles are assigned to group members who act out problem situations in human relations, without a script. The purpose of role playing, as a means of providing a reality base for personal understanding and insights for group discussion and training, is enlarged upon; and we see how a readiness for role playing may be created.

Before roles may be played there is a need for much sound preparation. This is described in detail as the method of selecting and designing the problem unfolds, and as the situation to be enacted is established. Characters are cast and briefed and the setting is created. It is in these chapters that one sees the difference between haphazard role playing done for a lark and the use of role playing as a sensitive device for leadership and group training. Much role playing that one sees today suffers from a lack of sound planning and preparation.

Because of the nature of our purposes the entire membership is to be involved and this phase of the method is discussed and illustrated in detail in Chapter 5. You will find new and exciting techniques, evolved from rich experience, related here.

A complete chapter is devoted to the leader of role playing so that one may assume that obligation with knowledge and some feeling of security. How to do this is the central focus.

The later part of the book is devoted to a comprehensive listing and description of how role playing may be used in many types of situations and organizations, with full illustrations, the values of the method, and ways to avoid dangers.

Although this was designed as a how-to-do-it book, the philosophy and principles of leadership training, human relations, and problem solving were not neglected. They serve to draw the book together and to make of it more than just a guide to techniques.

The book was written for members—of all organizations, everywhere. We have much in common in our group problems. It was written in the hope that the ideas and illustrations would be helpful to members who wished to train themselves and their fellow members in better methods for solving group problems.

ALAN F. KLEIN

University of Pittsburgh
Pittsburgh, Pennsylvania

Contents

Role Playing in Leadership Training and Group Problem Solving

CHAPTER 1

Using Role Playing in Your Meeting

Role playing is one of our newest tools for improving meetings, conferences, and leadership-training sessions. The idea is so natural and so simple that it is surprising that we had not thought of it before. Children have been role-playing for years. "Let's play house. You be the father and I'll be the mother and Jenny will be our daughter," or "Let's play store. You must come in to buy the food." And so on it goes, you be so-and-so, I'll be so-and-so, and we will play roles. It was not until Dr. J. L. Moreno of the Psychodramatic Institute in New York introduced methods which he called "psychodrama" and "sociodrama" that role playing for adults as a human relations training method came into its own.

Of course, even that is not strictly true. Industrial firms and department stores had been training salesmen, for example, by having their employees act out make-believe sales interviews with each other as a means of practice for their jobs. Such methods have been effective and successful. In recent years role playing has become popular in other fields.

When Moreno developed his techniques he was interested in therapy for certain kinds of personality disorders and this he called "psychodrama." His "sociodrama" was a method for testing ideas before putting them into actual use, as in the training of the salesmen we were talking about. It is this idea that has developed into role playing.

Role playing takes place when a group watches other members enact roles in a skit for the purpose of analyzing some real life situation in which it is interested. The performance is followed by discussion. The skit may present a situation so that the audience can be helped to understand what happens or happened in a given circumstance. The main point is that role playing is used to make a situation, problem, or incident real and thereby to make it possible for the group to understand it and to discuss or cope with it.

> The central idea of role playing lies in the assignment of roles to various members of the group who act out the problem situation in human rela-

> tions, usually without a script. The role-playing scene is followed by group discussion and possibly the scene is replayed with variations of personnel or circumstances. The purpose of role playing is to provide a close-to-reality base for personal understanding and insights and for group discussion and training. To the extent to which the trainee is able to identify himself with the role-playing participants, he is better able to appraise his own actions toward others and their reactions to him.[1]

Role playing can be a powerful method. It introduces the actors as well as the observers to the situation with dramatic impact. It draws the group from a purely intellectual exercise into an emotional experience. The entire meeting is pulled into the stream of events which the members can then feel as well as hear about. To really involve persons only this emotional reaction can make it a meaningful experience. When the meeting is focused on a problem or incident to this extent, discussion follows easily and can have depth. We do not need, then, to be concerned with how to cope with apathetic members and uninteresting meetings. These difficulties need not arise.

Role playing has been called by some leaders

[1] Cleveland Public Library bibliography card on role playing, Feb., 1955.

"reality practice." In this sense role playing provides the opportunity for us to play at a part in a situation and to practice how to behave most effectively. Such an exercise is practice in human relations. One might liken this to scrimmage practice of the football team in its training sessions. The team play is perfected, mistakes are observed and corrected, and the players learn how to cope with the problems of the game. In our context role playing is useful to learn how to work with other people, how to handle ourselves, and to observe and correct our human relations mistakes as we practice coping with the problems of group life.

But role playing is not just a gimmick, a gadget, a technique to use for fun or to entertain. Nor is it something to use just because it stimulates discussion and makes the meeting interesting. Role playing is a sensitive and useful method and, like any other good method, it should be used appropriately and thoughtfully. One begins with thinking about the purposes of the meeting or conference. What do we hope to accomplish? Only when the objectives are clearly in mind is it possible to think of methods of achievement and to determine whether role playing will serve the purposes most effectively. Like many of our newer meeting techniques, it can be overdone if we do not plan our meeting carefully.

Examples of How to Use Role Playing

In using role playing we must begin with a clear idea of our objectives in employing it. You will design it for a specific purpose. This is true of most methods, but it is particularly true here. Unless you know what your goal is you cannot select the best method; unless you know where you want to go you cannot select your route. Too many groups may use buzz groups, role playing, observers, feedback, and other social inventions just for the sake of using them. We suggest that the main uses of role playing are these: (1) training in leadership and human relations skills; (2) training in sensitivity to people and situations; (3) the stimulation of discussion; (4) training in more effective group problem solving.

It might be useful to watch some demonstrations now to illustrate what role playing is and how it is done. Let us assume that the group is studying leadership. We know that it is concerned about domineering leadership and that it wants to discuss this phase of its organizational life. I am the role-playing director here and have the responsibility to introduce some content into the learning sessions. Please note that this is not a script. The lines were not written in advance. This record in smaller type actually happened and was taken while it was happening. The players were not told what to say. Interspersed are my own comments to explain to you the reader what I am doing, since a fuller verbatim report might take too much time and space for our purposes here.

I begin by introducing the idea of role playing and some elements of the situation to be studied.

> This morning I should like to demonstrate some ideas about leadership and rather than just starting off with a discussion it would be more interesting and useful if we had a common experience to examine. To do this, of course, I need your help. We are going to enact a short scene here and I will try to show something about leadership. I need a group to lead if I am to do this. Let me tell you the story first.
>
> I am a representative of a Service Club and I have some money to give away. My club cannot decide what project to undertake. I have called a meeting of the people in town who should know what our town needs. I have asked a representative of the Community Welfare group—and Mr. Jenkins, chairman of the Chest board, has come; a representative of a group of ladies interested in old folks—and Mrs. Secord is with us; someone from the Health League—and Miss Twitchell is here; and the recreation director, Jack Splane.

> I am going to chair the meeting and, as you can see, this group is going to be asked to suggest and agree upon a project for our Service Club. Who feels that he or she can play one of the parts? Who can identify with Mr. Jenkins—or any of the others?
>
> Of course, you know that the folks who are in these skits get the most out of the sessions; and, also, I guarantee that no one will be embarrassed or subjected to ridicule or criticism. The one part that might call for some criticism I will take myself. I will be the leader.

Now I call for the players again. I stop talking and I do not plead or coax. I allow time for people to think and for the silence to take its effect. Because I know that players will come up, I am relaxed and secure. I show no sign of anxiety or pressure. I may say in a minute, "Now, who will be Mr. Jenkins?" I may say in certain instances, if people look too comfortable, "I really do not want to assign the roles." Sometimes someone says, "Joe, how about you doing Jenkins?" Then I say, "Let's not volunteer for someone else, eh? Who will do Jenkins?" I may drop Jenkins for the moment and say, "How about Mrs. Secord or Miss Twitchell?" I try not to talk too much and am willing to let the silence prompt people to volunteer.

As each part is spoken for, I thank the person

and, when all parts are filled, I invite them up to the front of the room. At this point I proceed to "warm them up." This process will be described later. Once we are warmed up I repeat the situation and the purpose of the meeting.

In the following statement I prepare my audience for involvement in the discussion to follow the role playing by saying to the audience, while my actors can hear also:

> I am going to change my leadership behavior several times during this skit. All the people on the left side of the room, watch me. Try to see when I change and be prepared to identify the behavior that makes you aware of the change. You people on the right, watch the players. Try to guess what they are feeling or how they are reacting. You people here in the center, watch specifically for the decision-making process. Let's play "hot and cold." See when we come close to consensus or a decision and when we seem to move apart, and try to figure out why. Is everyone clear? Are there any questions?

Now I help my committee to enact the scene realistically by saying:

> The value of what we are about to do lies in our trying to simulate the real thing. Let's try to act just as you think these people would act in this situation. Be as flexible or as rigid as you think

they would be. If you will try not to "ham" it or drop out of character I think you will enjoy it more. And please play a part—don't caricature someone we all know. Fine! Let's begin.

The actual role playing follows:

CHAIRMAN: Ladies and gentlemen, I have asked you to come here today to help us to help you. Service Club is looking for a project, and you are the people who should know what needs to be done in Urban Centre. We want your advice—but not a long list of needs. We have lists. What we want is one project that you agree is *the* need. Mind you, we have ideas of our own. We may not take your suggestion, if I do not think it advisable. The price range is around $3,000. What will it be?

MR. JENKINS: The Chest committee has gone into this, Mr. Chairman. The big welfare need in Urban Centre is for a Mental Health Clinic. We have surveyed the whole situation.

CHAIRMAN: If this is so important, Mr. Jenkins, why hasn't the Chest set up one?

MR. JENKINS: Money. We have no money for any extension of our services. We have not reached our objectives for the last three years.

CHAIRMAN: Sounds like a poor show to me. If we need a Clinic, that is certainly a Chest problem or one for the city fathers.

MRS. SECORD: It would be awfully nice, Mr. Chairman, if Service Club were to show interest in our older people—Senior Citizens. You know, they should have a club building of their own. Why, now you see them just going to the stores and sitting in the railway station because they have nowhere else to go. Now if. . . .

CHAIRMAN: That's fine, Mrs. Secord. Any others?

MR. SPLANE: Mr. Chairman, what we *need* is a decent play field and park. Think of it—Service Club Park. Every kid in Urban Centre would use it. Prevent Juvenile Delinquency. And maybe for once we could coach a winning team if we had a place to practice.

CHAIRMAN: That isn't the kind of thing I had in mind. Take the Motor Club. They are supporting Cerebral Palsy—and the Indians have a camp—and the Queensmen's run the TB survey. Something like that.

MISS TWITCHELL: Yes, Mr. Chairman, that's what I had in mind. . . .

CHAIRMAN: Well, sorry, I have no more time, I have a lunch appointment at the Club. Many thanks to you. Can we get together next week? I'll send out notices.

Leader: That was fine. Now let's forget everything we have seen or done and do this scene all over from the beginning.

We redo the scene with the leader changing his approach to demonstrate how the others will react to a different atmosphere.

CHAIRMAN: Good morning. It was good of you to come. I am Joe Carter and I think I know most of you here. On my left is Mrs. Secord from the Auxiliary of the Old Folks' program; next to her, Miss Twitchell of the Health League. You know Mr. Jenkins, chairman of the Chest board, and over here Jack Splane, our energetic recreation director. I know that you are busy people, so let's get down to the purpose of our being here. Service Club is looking for a project. We need your help. You are the people who know what Urban Centre needs and we have $3,000 to pay for it. We want you to choose the one thing for us.

MISS TWITCHELL: Mr. Chairman, I do appreciate being asked. Our concern is with health and we think health would be improved if we had a big educational campaign with posters and films and speakers. This would. . . .

MR. JENKINS: Miss Twitchell, don't you think we need a Mental Health Clinic first? You know the Chest board has surveyed the health needs and set that as a priority. Dr. Stevens of Health League was on that committee.

MISS TWITCHELL: I think the public must be educated to it first, don't you, Mr. Chairman?

CHAIRMAN: (*Nods*)

JACK SPLANE: As for me, I think health would be improved if people got more exercise. There isn't a decent field in town. As for mental health—recreation is the answer to that one. Prevention—and you don't need cure. Service Club Park and Playfield! There's the real need.

CHAIRMAN: (*Nods*)

MISS TWITCHELL: I can't say that I agree. It is fine to have fun and games, but people need doctors, too. As part of an educational campaign we would stress prevention, and recreation would be included, Mr. Splane.

CHAIRMAN: (*Smiles*)

MRS. SECORD: Where do the old folks come in?

CHAIRMAN (*changing behavior again*): I wonder if I might come in. Everything that you have said has been interesting and valuable to us. Seems that we need some principles or criteria upon which to base a choice. Let's use a blackboard and try to list some guides to our thinking. Upon what basis would you suggest that Service Club make a choice?

MISS TWITCHELL: Need. Where is the need?

CHAIRMAN: Yes. True enough. How do we assess need?

MR. JENKINS: On facts. What are the facts?

CHAIRMAN: Now we are all getting some place.

MR. SPLANE: Maybe we have to go out and ask the people what *they* think.

MR. JENKINS: Splendid idea.

CHAIRMAN: Does it seem that a survey or study is our first need?

At this point we cut the enactment because it has served our purpose.

And so on goes our meeting. This was, of course, a condensed version of what happened, just to illustrate the point. We use no script or rehearsal in role playing. The players were in roles; they were not themselves. They were not told how to act or what to say. Their performances were spontaneous. The situation was planned. I wanted to demonstrate three types of leadership so that the group could compare them, assess the results, and identify the leadership behavior involved. To be sure that this happened I set the entire plan. I might have asked three persons to assume the leadership in sequence. I could not be sure of what might result. I could have instructed each to demonstrate different behavior but, even then, I would have been planning the role playing to achieve desired results.

Now you have seen how I introduced the role playing and instructed the players, and what took place. This would be followed by group discussion and an analysis of the leadership approaches and the advantages, disadvantages, and skills involved. In the illustration just given, I as the leader selected both the situation and the roles. Now let us look at another approach.

The Group Plans the Situation

If the role playing is intended to communicate information, set a social problem, or interpret a report, it certainly can be planned in advance. This does not mean scripted and rehearsed. One of the requirements is that the action be spontaneous and natural. Let us look at this illustration of a planned role play, here planned not by the leader but by the members of the group.

The staff of a local recreation association was having its annual conference. The committee wanted to discuss the jobs of various staff members, and it was decided to role-play each one so that by showing the situation, discussion would follow naturally. A volunteer committee was drawn from the audience. It had one hour to plan for the evening session. The dialogue that follows is the planning for the role playing.

LEADER: We want to discuss the job of the "field representative." What do you think is his most typical daily problem?

MR. A: Handling a community conflict, I'd say.

LEADER: What do you think?

MR. G: That is certainly an everyday situation, but it must be more specific.

MR. F: It isn't that so much, as I see it. It is how to avoid giving advice and yet helping. (*All nod.*)

LEADER: I see nods. Is that the real problem?

(*All nod.*)

LEADER: I see. It is avoiding giving direct advice but

helping them to solve the conflict. What kind of conflict?

MR. G: Well, I have one now. The Tarsal Region want to foster a community center, and several big business men want an arena. The Tarsal Region want me to come down and help them settle this. Now, I can't go in and just advise them to build a center.

MR. A: Just tell them what happened in Luxen.

LEADER: Is this a good situation to illustrate our point?

(*Nods from all*)

LEADER: Mr. G, could you tell us more?

MR. G: Well, there is Glover. He owns the athletic goods and sports store. He is a snappy-salesman type who is pushing the arena. He outfits several teams for advertising now. He likes kids, but he has his eye on business mainly.

LEADER: How can we put this across?

MR. F: The "field rep" is driving to Tarsal. He is thinking about the problem, and he talks out loud and tells the audience what they must know.

MR. A: The size of the town, some history, who the key people are, and so on.

MR. F: Yes, and what he thinks about this.

LEADER: And how he feels?

MR. F: Yes, how he feels about going into this mess; where he would stand but also that he must not give advice.

MR. G: Well, if it were I, I'd be planning on whom I'd

see when I got to town. I'd want to see the recreation director, the chairman of the committee that runs recreation, someone from the City Council, and Rev. James Blunt.

MR. F: Don't forget Glover.

LEADER: Anyone else?

MR. A: Yes, the sponsors for the center.

MR. G: Sure, there is an old gal who is in just about everything in town. She's it.

LEADER: Whom does he see first?

SEVERAL: The recreation director and chairman.

LEADER: Before the officers of the Tarsal Region?

MR. A: Yes. He needs the information before he sees them.

LEADER: Where does this lead us?

MR. G: To a meeting. We have to stage a meeting of the Tarsal Region. Let's have everyone in that. This is where the "rep" must show what he would do.

LEADER: How does that sound?

(*Murmurs of assent*)

LEADER: Do we want to ask a "field rep" to do this? It's a lot to ask.

MR. A: I wouldn't mind doing it if the boss weren't there, but that makes it tough. Let's ask Ed to do it. He has nothing to lose since he's the drama chairman.

LEADER: O.K. How about this? When the meeting is over we'll do a flashback and ask various people what their reaction to the "rep" was and why?

MR. G: That's good. I think that is what we really want to know.

LEADER: Let's cast it. Who will do what . . . , etc.?

This was not role playing but a verbatim report of how a planning committee worked up the situation to be role-played. You may be interested in noting the way in which the leader helped the group to plan the situation by asking questions appropriately.

The Situation Arises in the Discussion

MRS. JONES: I think it is her own fault. If she didn't stand for such treatment her husband wouldn't do what he does.

MRS. ALLEN: What would you suggest that she do? Leave him?

MRS. JONES: No. Give him some of his own back.

MRS. ROLAND: That couldn't work, Mrs. Jones. Believe me, I know. You have to put yourself in his place. Why does he act as he does?

MR. CHRISTIE: It might be because of job frustration—he may be a square peg in a round hole.

LEADER: Could she help him, do you think?

MR. CHRISTIE: She could if she understood him better.

MRS. ROLAND: I say she could help him if she gave him some feeling that he was somebody.

LEADER: Maybe we could try a few of these theories out. Let's enact it from the two suggested points of view and see what solutions we get and how she might help herself and her husband.

Here the situation arises right in the discussion. The scene has been set by the discussion, and we are ready to test our theories. In the enactment above we get the story first and then enact it. In the example to follow we get the story through the enactment:

MRS. A: What I want to know is this. How do you handle a member who is always complaining? Everything is wrong. Everyone is wrong. It is discouraging.

MRS. M: What does she complain about?

MRS. A: Everything. The refreshments, the music, the speaker, the dues, the constitution–everything.

LEADER: Let's get a picture of this lady. Would you be able to act her out so that the rest of us could see what you are up against? Someone else will be you.

We act it out. Then we discuss how it might be handled. Then we act out the suggested methods of dealing with the problem. It might happen this way:

The previous discussion has gone on. The leader asks the meeting how they might advise Mrs. A.

MRS. Z: I'd just tell her I was fed up and if she didn't like it she could quit.

LEADER: That is one solution. Would you come up and do it for us so that we can see how you would tell her and what might result?

Or this way:

The previous discussion has gone on. The leader asks the meeting how they might advise Mrs. A.

MRS. Z: I would . . .

LEADER: Don't tell us. Show us. Would you come up and do it for us so that we can see how?

Or this way:

MR. CABLE: After our last discussion I thought I saw the point. I tried it and—poof! It fell flat.

LEADER: What happened?

MR. CABLE: We were discussing how committee members won't take responsibility because the chairman doesn't give them a chance. I said to myself, that's me. From now on I won't talk or do the jobs for them. So what happened? No one said anything, and I *had* to talk.

LEADER: Would you like to role-play it, so maybe we can see what might have gone wrong?

MR. CABLE: Sure.

LEADER: Who would be willing to be Mr. Cable? He can brief you and act as consultant to you while we do this. Fine. Now, Mr. Cable, can you tell us what the situation was?

Notice here that we are protecting Mr. Cable from being himself. He is role-playing.

Now that we have seen several examples of role playing, we are ready to examine, in greater detail, the principles of how to do it.

In the chapters to come let us go through the following steps that are customarily followed in using role playing:

a. Defining the problem
b. Creating a readiness for role playing
c. Establishing the situation
d. Casting the characters
e. Briefing and warming up
f. Considering the training design
g. Acting
h. Stopping
i. Involving the audience
j. Analysis and discussion
k. Evaluation

CHAPTER 2

Helping the Group to Role-Play

Problem solving and leadership training are most effective when the problems and situations worked upon arise from the needs and interests of the group. Since this is so, the conference plan, meeting plan, or institute plan should be based upon what the participants want and need. They will want to work on problems that have interest and meaning for them and will learn most in this way.

There is reason to believe that role playing also is more successful if the situation being enacted is of concern to the actors and the audience. Therefore it is important for us to determine how to discover and define the problems, or to note in what aspects of leadership and human relations our group requires training.

This book is about a method for training. The trend today in adult training seems to point clearly in the direction of self-motivated learning, around problem solving. There would be little value in role playing as a method, therefore, if the problems enacted were not real ones to the group. There is a realization that in the past too often the teacher or leader chose the course content and the problems. This tended to reduce interest and involvement of the members and hence lessened the amount learned. Today we work on the concerns of the members and we encourage self-motivated learning and self-training.

In addition, because of the nature of role playing it would seem most appropriate that the situations enacted be human relations situations.

Defining the Problem

There are various ways to determine what situations to role-play. One way might be for a representative committee of the participants to meet to discuss their interests, needs, and priorities. Such a committee seeks to define the real problems and hence focus the sessions to follow. Another method might be to convene a meeting of an executive group to discuss the needs of the members. The executive group might have discussed the question with their own members previously or might select the problems without such prior investigation. Still another method might be to convene a meeting of the older organizational heads to discuss what new members ought to know and be taught.

In many instances it seems preferable to ask the group to assess its own needs and to suggest its own problems around which the members require training. This method is recommended widely for human relations training today, but a word of caution is needed. This is not so simple or so sound as many would have us believe. People very often do not know what they need; they have not diagnosed their own behavior or lacks. They do, however, usually know what bothers them, and this is a starting point. But some do not know even that. They have no problems, they believe, because they do not know enough about it to know that there is a problem. This situation is not so usual with reference to groups but it is common among individuals in those groups. A group discussion helps such people to begin to see that nothing is so perfect that it cannot be improved upon, and to readjust their sights.

The group can be stimulated to diagnose its concerns. Picture a session such as one that might develop in your organization if we began by listing our goals, objectives, and purposes on the blackboard. To list would not be helpful enough so we would discuss them as we put them down. Then the leader might ask for a listing of the values upon which the objectives rested. This is more difficult. We are having to think. We are not all in accord, either. That calls for discussion and illustration on the part of the discussants. Experiences and events begin to come to consciousness. Problems are emerging. Suppose now the leader asks what obstacles stand in our way that prevent us from reaching our goals or fulfilling them to the extent that we might wish, or as fast as we might wish, and what we see as examples of those blockages. Can we ask now whether we would like to find some solutions to these problems? Or perhaps what skills are needed to cope with such problems, or what skills are needed to do certain tasks or jobs? In this way we can bring the needs and problems to light.

Some problems just arise in the discussion as natural outcroppings of the subjects being discussed or as naturally out of the frustrations that the group may have with its own progress or operation. For instance, in a group which is discussing equal pay for equal work for women, one person feels that the group needs more information on equality. Another feels that the group knows the problem exists but that the real problem is apathy among women themselves. Others feel that it is a case of what can one do about it anyway, and hence apathy. Someone says that it seems to be a matter of how to deal with indifference born of hopelessness. There is assent. The leader then suggests that the group try to make this more specific so that a situation can be acted out, and a real situation is examined to see what is involved.

Another method is to canvass the group by mail before the conference or meeting and ask about its concerns. If asked as baldly as that, the responses may be guarded, superficial, or not forthcoming. Let us see whether we can ask in a somewhat more useful manner:

> Please give one example of a typical situation in your chapter that annoyed you, and of one that pleased you very much.
>
> Describe one person with whom you find it difficult to deal.
>
> Give an illustration of a troublesome incident and how it was handled. Do you think it was well handled, or poorly handled? Why?
>
> What do you consider to be the most important subject for discussion at our forthcoming meeting?
>
> What would you most like to learn about or how to do at the sessions?
>
> What do you think most of the members need to work on for self-improvement?
>
> Describe in some detail a case you would like to have discussed.

It is not suggested that you use all or any of these questions, but these are offered as examples of how one might go about discovering the needs or interests of a group for preconference or premeeting planning and might use this information to design role playing for appropriate places.

A problem census can be made at the meeting. In this method the members begin by listing problems and problem areas in human relations and then deciding what they want to talk about. Though much is made of this approach in many articles on the subject, some are skeptical. This problem census can be used to warm up a group, to show them that you do plan to talk about things that concern them, and to get some clues about them. This is useful when you do not know the group too well. If you use it you will find that the problems raised tend to be vague and general. You must help the group to be specific. This can be done by asking for a concrete example, by asking for elaboration, or by indicating that you do not know the situation well enough and would the person who suggested it please explain further. To do this properly takes a lot of time.

It is well not to rely upon this method because persons usually do not offer their real problems at once. They will not risk themselves to that extent so soon. Real human relations problems are often below the level of consciousness. People like to tell you what they think you expect to hear. Often an articulate person offers his personal problems, pet "beefs," or things that have been discussed before.

When a group is uncomfortable because of its own interpersonal relations or because of its relations with its leader it may seek to escape into the clouds and talk about theoretical and fancy-sounding ideas. It may also indulge itself in listing many problems and push off getting down to working on any one of them. When the group is asked to select the problem it wants to tackle it may spend too much time on this aspect of the session.

If the leader cuts the census short some good suggestions may never be made, or the suggestions selected may not be very important. If the census drags on too long the group may become bored, things may be repeated, the list may look too imposing and hence become discouraging, or the possibility of doing anything useful may seem remote. One good thing here is that if the census seems to be unproductive it gives the group something to talk about right off—why are we having this trouble?

If a census is made, the next step is to consolidate the list into broader categories, for surely the things listed will bear some relationship to each other. Some may be parts of others, or depend upon others. This can be done by the leader and group together, or by the leader with the approval of the group. The latter seems preferable. Some leaders like to take the list away with them and use it themselves to consolidate and plan the next session. This, too, has some merit.

After the list is consolidated the group may be asked to express its preferences for immediate work by a quick show of hands but no discussion on each item. In this way we can attempt to be sure that we shall be working on things that really interest the group. But a word of caution. Don't be too sure! People usually blame everyone but themselves for their problems. They resist training. They test leaders. They are not always good barometers of their own stormy weather. In matters like this, some prefer a less direct approach than a problem census.

If you know the group or are part of it you know that the extent to which the members are free to work on real problems depends upon the relationships within the group. When do we "let our hair down," and with whom? The keys to problem identification, then, rest upon the atmosphere in intimate groups. Is there fear of reprisal, ridicule, and punishment (social as well as other) for expressing problems or concern? Are there rewards or status to persons who are seen as helping the group, or are people seeking *status quo* and willing to let the sleeping dogs lie?

Once these questions have been resolved in your planning and you have selected what you believe to be the problems that are of concern to most of the members of the group they should be phrased so as to be specific, concrete, simple, and actable. Now we are ready to go on to the next step.

In order to use role playing the group may be helped to want to role-play through an appreciation of the purpose and a desire for the end result. How can we create a readiness for role playing?

Creating a Readiness for Role Playing

We shall assume now that our group is interested in human relations and in leadership training and that the problem upon which it is working is real, also that the problem would lend itself to role playing. The leader would explain what role playing is, if the group had not used it before. He might then discuss why it would be useful in dealing with the problem at hand. Even with a group that has role-played before, it is advantageous to explain why it would be a good method to use at the time. For example:

> I should like to suggest that we role-play this situation. Just talking about the problem does not

> seem to give us all that we need. If we could see it I am sure that it would become clearer.

In another context one might say:

> This question involves a matter of skill that can be acquired best by doing rather than talking. I suggest that we role-play it so that you can practice how to handle this kind of situation.

To reduce the feeling against acting in front of other people, start a group role-playing something familiar, simple, and nonthreatening. This can be done by having everyone role-play at the same time, with no audience, since everyone is acting. This method is described later under the heading of multiple role playing. You could introduce role playing to your group by showing the film "Role Playing" [1] or the films "Invisible Committees" [1] or "Meeting in Session." [2]

When introducing role playing, as much threat reduction as possible should be included. That is, you explain that no one will be ridiculed or judged, that those who participate will get the most out of it; that it is enjoyable and that everyone in the session is there to learn. One might say, also, that it is

---

[1] "Role Playing" and "Invisible Committees" can be secured from National Education Association, 1201 Sixteenth St., N.W., Washington 6, D.C.

[2] "Meeting in Session": Center for Improving Group Procedure, Teachers' College, Columbia University, New York, N. Y.

better to make mistakes here in a protected setting while making believe than to make them out in real life where you have "to play for keeps." Another protection is that no one is playing himself and since he is in a role he can experiment with how to act in the situation without any fears. It is well to focus any tension about role playing onto the problem, "We want to solve this problem pretty badly. Let's try to solve it. Let's role-play it."

The person doing the leading must be warm, relaxed, and easy. He must expect that the group will respond. He should make it easy for people to be themselves, to speak freely, to act as they would with friends, to be involved and participating.

We have now selected and defined the problem and created a readiness to approach its solution through role playing.

CHAPTER 3

Preparing for Role Playing

Before we can enact our role play we must prepare for it. We do this by establishing the situation so that it is actable and so that the points to be learned will be brought out, by casting the characters, and by briefing and warming up the players.

Establishing the Situation

Let us examine these preliminary steps in some detail since successful role playing depends upon proper preparation. First of all, the situation needs to be considered.

To Work on a Problem Situation

If the purpose of the role playing is to work on a problem that is situation-centered, the roles of the actors should be defined, but the situation can be left open to allow the group freedom to explore it.

An example may make this clearer. If the group is discussing juvenile delinquency and its control, the problem may be centered on the subject and not primarily on the behavior of the role players. In this case, if the situation is too carefully structured the role players will have no scope in which to explore the problem or seek solutions. However, the players must be prepared to know just who they are and what their relation to each other is in order to be free to center their attention on the problem. For example:

> In a middle-size midwestern city the delinquency rate has been rising. Some children have been put in jail, but it has not seemed to help. The children of better-class families have become involved in delinquent behavior, and the residents have become concerned. The police say that they cannot handle the problem without the help of the parents.
>
> A committee has been called by the Council to consider the problem and to suggest solutions. Some facts are that 30 per cent of the adolescents have been in some trouble with the police in the last year. Fifteen per cent have been punished through some form of court action. Most of this 15 per cent come from broken homes or blighted

areas. In these areas there is little play space and there is unemployment.

We are about to role-play the committee in order to explore the problem, and not to focus on the human relations behavior of the players.

We have given the framework of a situation, but there is leeway for the role players to explore the causes of delinquency, discuss possible solutions that they know have been tried, and go on to problem solving. The purpose here is to involve the group in the question of delinquency, to encourage maximum participation, and to stimulate discussion; therefore we define the roles carefully but do not structure the problem.

The committee consists of the following characters (note how the roles are set):

Mrs. McKee—a laywoman of a fine family. She is interested, hardworking, willing, well informed.
Judge Brown—Juvenile Court judge. He is old, steady, conservative, kindly, and worried about the problem.
Joe Runner—a representative of the Recreation Committee.
A. Leaf—the high school principal.
Miss Kotter—case supervisor of the Department of Public Welfare.
Al Lund—the chairman. He believes in the demo-

> cratic process but he also believes that problems have solutions; that if facts are put together in an orderly fashion the parts will match and the answer will be obvious.

We cast the kind of roles that are normal or usual in such a situation. We are not looking for conflict or special problems of resistance but just a discussion of the delinquency situation.

In such a situation we can look in addition at how the chairman approaches the chairmanship job, also how the member roles shape up, and how an ordinary group tackles a problem. With just the information we have revealed thus far, the group can role-play for the purposes stated.

But let us suppose that we had a somewhat different purpose, namely to show that members in such a situation resist facts and like to make decisions on their own without recourse to the facts. Observe how we proceed to establish each situation in accordance with the purpose for the role playing.

We might leave the situation as it is but now further set the roles. We might instruct the chairman as follows:

> You like to get things done logically and systematically and see an orderly sequence to tackling this problem. Present a proposed agenda.
>
> 1. Diagnosis of the problem and the situation
> 2. Plan of action

3. Taking first step toward solution
   Try to discourage the group from going on to a plan until you think the facts are revealed and the problem analyzed.

To facilitate this demonstration you might give each of the players a few more facts about delinquency in town or bring them out in the warm-up session. You might also tell the players more about their own jobs or bring it out in the warm-up so that they would have personal points of view. For example you might say to each of the players:

Mrs. McKee: Your husband believes that this is a problem for the police and should be left right there. You do not know about that but you do know that the board of the Children's Society on which you serve does not have enough money to do its job.

Judge Brown: Here are more facts about numbers, types of offenses, trends, and ages that you can make use of in your comments: . . .

Joe Runner: Remind the committee that you have not been given the use of the schools for recreational purposes.

A. Leaf: The point that kids need discipline is a "natural" for you.

Miss Kotter: You could describe the wretched conditions of one area of the city and the increasing case load, such as. . . .

You need not worry about whether people will try to get at facts. Unless you have a trained and able group it will disregard facts in almost all cases and plow on to premature conclusions. If this does not happen, either your group did not need this lesson or by it they will have learned that facts are essential, and this could be brought out in the discussion.

But you might establish the situation a bit differently if you wished to expose the group to the idea that people have preconceived solutions and are idea possessive. You might, for example, instruct each player, privately, that he had a point of view.

Mrs. McKee: You believe there is a lack of spiritual and moral training in the home.

Joe Runner: The cause of delinquency is a lack of recreational facilities. Of this you are convinced.

A. Leaf: You believe that there is an abysmal lack of respect for the law.

Miss Kotter: You know that the cause of all this is broken homes.

Now with the same situation we can show how groups react to different chairmanship roles. The leader can assume different approaches as in the illustration given earlier. He can brief several persons by giving them different instructions, such as these:

Chairman 1: You are a busy man and you like to get things done. This is the way you run your business. There is not time for endless discussion. You pride yourself on starting on time and going through the entire agenda (no matter how long) in one hour. Besides, this problem is an easy one; if only all were so easy. The solution is–it is up to the schools and churches to handle the kids; let's give them the job and the authority to do it.

Chairman 2: You are personally committed to the concept of democratic leadership with its counterpart, shared leadership. You are willing to allow the group plenty of time for exploration and you know the value of a friendly, warm meeting atmosphere.

Chairman 3: You are a "born leader" with no qualms about manipulation. You have a solution up your sleeve but you will not reveal it. You will try subtly to influence the group in your direction. Friendly, warm, jovial, and disarming, you put it over.

Notice that in each of these illustrations the problem has been left unchanged and unstructured. We have changed merely the roles. These are examples only of how the situation may be established and used to experience different leadership. The chairman may be changed while the action proceeds, in sequence, or the enactment may be redone with a different leader each time.

Another approach might be to select seven persons at random and just change chairmen periodically without any special instructions. (The number seven has no magical significance.)

Although the problem posed may not be the best for the following purpose, we shall use it here to make a point. Suppose we wanted to show how subgroups form or how prestige or status affects meetings. We might establish the situation with slight variations by a few new role factors:

> *Mrs. McKee:* You and your husband are very highly regarded in this community. Mr. McKee plays golf with Judge Brown. The Judge has been in your home many times and hopes your husband will back him in his next political rise.
>
> *Judge Brown:* You and Mr. McKee are good friends. McKee has promised to back you for a very desirable advancement. You have been in the home of the McKees often. In fact, it was McKee who got you your present post.
>
> *Joe Runner:* Mrs. McKee and Judge Brown are very influential people. It would pay you to cultivate them. Al Lund used to play hockey with you.
>
> *A. Leaf:* Mrs. McKee is a very influential person in town. Runner is an upstart. He is causing trouble by raising the issue of use of school buildings again. Al Lund is a very fine person. You

hope he will be on your side because he has a reputation for being a go-getter and winner.

Miss Kotter: You do not know any of these people, except the Judge. You have never been impressed by the Judge but you do have to work with him. Runner does nothing useful in your area. You know about Mrs. McKee but you do not go for the type.

A few more role points added, and you could show conflict. It is not hard to see how.

If you wished to show vested interest, each of these people could be representatives of organizations with axes to grind, points of view, or with no authority to commit their groups.

Where the purpose is to *depict* a social problem, the social situation should be as well defined as possible.

With a little ingenuity you can adjust or alter the roles you pose to the purpose desired. Many of the illustrations above can be combined in various ways to suit your particular use. You could, I am sure, think up many other adaptations.

To Work on Human Relations

Where the purpose is to focus on how individuals function, as in skills training, insight production, or human relations, the roles are left more flexible but the situation is well defined. Here we want to allow the people wide scope for behaving as they think the role should be done but within a situation well-enough structured that they know at what they are working. The skills role may be left relatively free, and the other roles may be developed so as to test or reveal the skill. Some roles are just part of the situation itself. Here is an example of how we prepare for this by structuring the situation:

> *Miss Fulton*—the skills role: You have been working in an office for nine years as a secretary. Because girls come and go, as the senior person you do most of the breaking in and arranging of schedules and so on. Part of your time is spent on this supervisory job, but for the most part you are a secretary as they are. You are not listed as a supervisor, but you get more money than the others. You like the arrangement, pay, and conditions.
>
> Christmas holidays are coming up, and the plant is very busy. A skeleton shift is going to work over the holidays. You are asked to get one of the girls to stay on to do whatever small amount of work will be required. She will be paid double time. You have arranged a meeting with the girls to discuss it. You expect strong resistance because no one likes to work holidays, or to work alone, and the amount of money involved is small. They do not have to work if they don't want to, but if you fail to get someone to work it will jeopardize

your position since you hope to be selected as office manager soon. Also, you had planned to go home for Christmas week and all arrangements are made, so you do not want to work yourself. Before the meeting you have thought up some ideas of how to approach the girls. Think over what their attitudes are likely to be and how to deal with them.

It is the situation you have described. The role player will have to make up the personality and behavior of Miss Fulton. Here the actor is completely free.

To those who are to take the parts of the girls:

Girl No. 1: You have been working in this office for a year. It is reasonably satisfactory, but the pay is small and the Christmas bonus was disappointing. You have been looking forward to Christmas holidays because a certain boy will be coming into town.

Girl No. 2: You have been working in this office for two months. You like it and you want to stay. You do not like the girl who seems to take on the office management but was never given the authority so far as you know. You do not have any special plans for Christmas but you sure don't like to be pushed around by these other girls. You would do them a favor if they gave you something worth while in return.

> *Girl No. 3:* You have been working in this office for five months. You are on the desk and switchboard and you hate it. You wish you were on straight secretarial work but you don't take shorthand. A promotion would be just what you want. The office supervisor could put in a good word for you but did she not put No. 2 into a job recently when you had been there longer? Should you be nice and play it safe or give her a bit of her own?

Our emphasis here will be on how the supervisor handles the problem. We shall not be misled by the content or situation but shall concentrate on the role of the supervisor and what she reveals about behavior and human relations.

You will be able to see dozens of ways of building a situation to show interpersonal relations, hostility, or conflict. There are many ways in which to handle it. Chairmanship behavior can be revealed, portrayed, or tested as can other leadership roles. Interracial situations can be staged with the question of how one handles oneself, copes with the problem, or corrects it as the focus.

Another method of establishing the situation is to tell a story and ask the group to play out how it might have been handled at the end. Here we may be concerned with either the problem or the behavior or both. For example:

John Thompson was an active member of the Club. He had been a hard worker and a faithful one. John had a friend whom he liked very much and who had helped him on many occasions and in many ways. One open meeting night John asked his friend Ben to come down to the meeting. Ben did come and enjoyed it. Later, John and his wife asked Ben and his wife to a Saturday Night Open House of the Club and they had a wonderful time. Ben was introduced around and everyone was very friendly.

Ben was a distributor for Templar cars. Two members of the Club's finance committee called upon him to ask whether he would be willing to contribute to the Club, for its charity project of the year, the net profit on the next Templar he sold. When Ben heard the specific purpose of the project, he gave the Club a new Templar as a donation free of charge. The Club was delighted, and Ben was toasted and praised.

Ben told John he was becoming very much interested in the Club activities and wondered how he might help further. John promised to discuss this with Big Bill Sloan, the president. John invited Sloan and Ben to lunch without telling either what he had in mind. At lunch John asked Ben if he would like to join the Club. Ben said he would. Sloan looked very unhappy. John asked Sloan whether he would propose Ben. Sloan turned red and asked John why he did not do it

> himself. John said he thought Ben deserved the honor of being proposed by the president. Sloan said he would like to but he did not think he could. After all, he did not know Ben as well as John.
>
> At this point John got annoyed and asked Sloan what the trouble was. Sloan said, "Look, John, this is very embarrassing. Why did you not ask me before you invited me here? You have me on the spot. I do not want to hurt Ben here, I like Ben—but you know that we have a religious qualification for membership. I don't like it but I can't do anything about it."

The role playing begins now after the story has been told, and the group is asked to carry the situation on from here. What would Ben do? What should John do? Note here that the story defines the situation in detail but what Ben or John will do or even what kind of person each is, is left to the actor to develop. It is in this development that we shall study and examine human relations behavior.

It might be well to point out again that if insights and skills underlie the purpose in any of these instances, there must be opportunity for practice and testing of the new skills and insights. If the purpose is primarily to discuss, see the common situation, or analyze a problem, practice and testing are not essential. How to do this would seem obvious.

For example, if the simple skill is how to approach a resident to buy a ticket we do it over and over to practice how, and test our skill and ability in different situations.

How to Design Your Situations

In discussing the design for role playing we come into a most interesting and provocative area. Even with so new a method, different schools of thought have arisen with champions for each. In this book, we intend to present many approaches. You may take your choice.

The design of your role playing, like any other design, allows for your imagination, creative ability, and adjustment to the level of the group for which it is to be used. It will depend upon the skill that you acquire in using the tool appropriately.

It should be clear now that role playing may be a training device, or it may be a device to stimulate discussion and engage in problem solving. As a training device it may be used to learn a specific skill or to get insight into one's own or another's feelings. On the other hand it may coax out feelings which affect the members' and groups' behavior but which are not verbalized generally and may bring them before the group for examination. In other situations role playing is used to convey information, to communicate content, or to report.

Here now are the basic fundamentals that determine design.

Should the role playing be completely unplanned or should the situations be prepared in advance of the conference, meeting, or training session? Examples of both approaches were given in Chapter 1. Which is preferable?

The way it is to be done will be dependent upon the outcome desired or needed by the group at the time. We have several alternatives. The role playing may be planned in advance by the leader or person responsible for the session; it may be planned by a committee which has assessed in some suitable way the needs and interests of the group; it may be planned by a subcommittee to fit into a conference theme; a member or the leader can suggest an actual incident to be played; or the group can make up the situation at the meeting right there and then.

If the outcome desired is the learning of a specific skill or idea, then our goal or objective is clearly defined, and we have, in a sense, a curriculum or content to be learned. The leader or committee has material to introduce and is responsible to see that it gets done. It is appropriate, then, to have a plan and to be certain that the points to be taught are in the role-playing design so that they can be learned. Time is an important consideration.

When time is short or limited there is a greater need for advance planning and hence prefabricated role-playing situations. In all cases the situation should contain controversy or conflict, a problem or obstacle to overcome. This is the essence of all drama and, in fact, of all life. The actors by seeking solution or resolution are helped to learn.

The situation should have some element of challenge to the group in that it puts the group into a state of discomfort. If we are satisfied with the situation as it is, or if we are content with the way we do things we are not ready to learn, change, or move. Education begins when we are not satisfied with what we know or what we do. All real education is self-education, hence to change (educate-learn) ourselves we must want to be changed. A problem or conflict situation produces tension. To resolve the tension we seek solution and in so doing we live, grow, and learn.

You may be wondering what this has to do with you. All organizational life depends upon human relations. Every club or association member has his own ideas about human relations; about how to get along in the organization and how to conduct himself. To help make our organizational life more effective in meetings, committees, tasks, and all other phases means re-education in human relations to some degree.

Re-education in human relations means some change in behavior. In effect, all discussion in our groups in some way changes the attitudes, values, or ideas of the individual members. Were this not so, there would be little to recommend discussion or group life. The role-playing design should be challenging enough to hold interest, stimulate thinking, and motivate learning. It should not be so threatening as to immobilize, create extreme anxiety, or block learning because of intense resistance.

The design should not be highly complex. If it is too filled with plot and counterplot the actors and observers may become confused and led astray, or the points may be missed. It cannot hope to unfold too many learning experiences at the same time. It should not take the group's attention off the problem by introducing irrelevant facts or unnecessary description. It should have enough facts and content to make the situation live. If the purpose is to study how Jones handled himself, the group should not be distracted by an intriguing story in which they are misled into discussing the story and not Jones.

The situation should be specific, clear, and short. Clarity is of great importance. One must be sure always that all concerned understand the situation, the roles, the problem, and what they are trying to do. This means repetition and an invitation for people to ask questions if they are not sure. If the situation is simple, briefing may be done orally. If it is the least bit involved, instructions should be in writing.

The situation and design should be pitched to the level of the group. To do otherwise is fatal. The principle is fairly obvious. The practical application calls for careful planning and deliberation.

Casting the Characters

Casting can be arranged for most readily by the person directing the role playing. The group lacks sufficient insight usually into the purposes of the experience, and the needs of the persons, to do the casting.

It seems best to ask people to assume the roles rather than to assign them. People find it hard to perform in a role with which they cannot identify. If they cannot do it the reality is gone, and the other actors are thrown off their stride. Assigning roles is an imposition unless, and this is a big *unless*, it is a training group and people have agreed to this procedure because they are relying on a trainer who they think knows what experiences will be productive. It is believed that no one should be forced or be overly urged to do a role.

It is surprising how people will catch on to their own needs if the atmosphere is not threatening and if the interpretation is good. We were called upon recently to present role playing to a group about to retire from work. The purpose was to develop some insights into the problems of retirement and to look at some solutions. The role players met at dinner to plan the situations. They selected as one situation the person who is a perpetual crank and grouch, and how others react to him; and then the same scene with a person who is pleasant, and how others react to him. When the casting was being done one man agreed to be the grouch, and then he added that it would be easy for him because he was that way naturally. Someone else commented that it would do him good to play the pleasant person. He laughed it off. Twenty minutes later he seized upon a pause in the discussion to ask if he could change his role, "To see how it feels to be a lot of fun."

With a new group or one not used to role playing it is a help to start easily with very simple roles and ones that are quite familiar to the players and that offer no threats or real challenges. As the group becomes more adept and more secure in the idea, roles can be cast that cause people to stretch themselves.

There are some disadvantages to using people in roles for which they volunteer if one is interested in skill training primarily:

1. The easy and articulate people volunteer first and often need the experience least.
2. The ones who need the practice may not volunteer.
3. The volunteers may not choose roles that will help them most.
4. It is difficult to get people to volunteer for unpopular roles or difficult ones, or where they may reveal themselves.

In small groups everyone may be drawn into a role eventually, and so the first and second disadvantages are not serious. In large groups this is not true. Also, by the method of reversing roles on the redoing, the third disadvantage may be avoided. The leader may do the unpopular roles himself or ask high status persons in the group to do them. Lastly, the members of the audience can get insight by watching the role playing even if the onlookers are not in the act. If a group is using role playing for training itself over a period of time, all the disadvantages disappear by themselves. If it is being used at a conference or once at a meeting, perhaps we cannot expect that the one shot will produce miracles. Even here by redoing, testing, and discussing, some results may be achieved. Surely within the broader objectives many excellent results are accomplished.

Casting should not use the players' own names. Persons should not play themselves or their own roles except under very special situations as for personal diagnosis, or in advanced human relations training courses to test and practice. Even here it is desirable to play roles when role playing. It is preferable not to enact the actual event as it occurred except for diagnosis and here only if the persons are willing to open themselves for criticism. It is very possible to hurt people this way, undermine self-confidence and, one might add, lose friends. In our club life it is not recommended, and in personnel training it may be useful only if it is conducted in well-controlled educational conditions with top-notch trainers. Not under any circumstances would one recommend therapy in unskilled hands. Giving people more self-awareness than they can handle, with no out such as that it was a make-believe role, can prove damaging.

In some circumstances it is useful to help people assume roles to which they aspire and hence give them practice in something they may soon do or hope to do.

Some persons prefer neither to assign roles nor to ask for volunteers. In their method they staple the instructions for each role together in any order and hand the packet to the group instructing them to take the top one off and pass the set. Each plays the part he gets by chance.

Briefing and Warming Up

There have been numerous examples of briefing throughout these pages.[1] A short explanation may be sufficient here. Briefing may be oral or written. If the situation is quite simple the briefing may be done orally. The planner must decide how much he wants all or any of the parties to know. Again this depends upon the purpose of the role playing, what would be true to life, and how he sees the human relations aspect of the situation. Let us look at a few examples.

> A large organization or club holds monthly meetings for its membership. About a hundred persons attend. The chairman has been in office for many years and is a highly respected person. He always conducts meetings in strict accordance with the rules of parliamentary procedure. The meetings are very formal with committee reports and formal instructions. In addition, there is always a speaker who is formally introduced, the speech lasts forty minutes, there is a fifteen-minute question period, no more, a formal "thank you" speech and formal adjournment. In recent months attendance has fallen off, and people are registering feelings of discontent. A committee has been selected to study the drop in attendance and to

[1] See also p. 14, *How to Use Role Playing* (Chicago: Adult Education Association of the U.S.A., 1955, 48 pp.).

make recommendations to the total membership on what action might be taken.

This information is given to everyone. When the chairman is chosen for the role play he is asked to leave the room with the following written additional briefing information. We do not want the others to know this.

> You believe that the meeting problem can be solved by getting better speakers. Good speakers will have to be paid and that means an increase of membership dues. To do this the obvious answer is a membership drive. Another solution, in addition, is to have more publicity for the meetings. You have called the meeting of the committee to get its reactions to your suggestions although you did not make this explicit when you called it. (This, being unknown to the others, sets the stage for exploration and conflict. If you tell the others such things you are asking them to be actors, that is, to feign surprise or resentment, and the spontaneity is lost. If there are such hidden elements they can react *as they would in real life*, which is in fact just what we are trying to effect.)

If the players are to interact with each other in a reality situation there will be things that they do not know about each other's plans and feelings. However, if the purpose is to present a social situation scene, everyone might have to know the entire story because here even the interaction is to be planned. The point in this is, how many unknowns do you want the players to react to spontaneously in order to achieve the experience or demonstrate the learnings, and how much would they know or not know if this were happening in true life?

Each of the others gets the following written briefing note:

> One of you has been attending meetings of another organization. This organization does not use parliamentary procedure and it has eliminated name speakers except on rare occasions. It is this person's idea that a change in the procedure of conducting meetings is necessary to increase interest and hence attendance. (Three other committee members have their own ideas which they have not been given, and which will not be talked over among them. When the four leave the room with the briefing sheets they will select among themselves the one to be the proponent of changing the meetings.)
>
> All of you have discussed the problem but you have no group decision as to what recommendations are to be made. You assume that the meeting has been called to discuss the problem and to try to reach an agreement. You realize that the chairman will have to change his methods but

> that he cannot be forced, he must be convinced. He is a high-status person, respected by all the members of this committee and the organization.

So that the briefing here will be clear, what are the objectives underlying the role play? We are interested in getting a person who is tradition bound to want to try some different methods and to give up some old ones. In so doing we want to see what our committee members are up against and how each will handle himself, and especially how the one member who is to try to induce change will approach his role. In the play we shall hope that we will see how a committee analyzes the forces holding the chairman to tradition and how it builds counteracting forces; how it can help him to see that he can use other methods or can delegate to others the planning for other types of meetings and the advantages in such an idea; how it can help him to see that there is a cause-and-effect relationship between the drop in attendance and the way meetings are run.

In the illustration of the role play of a field representative given earlier (page 30), the planning group briefed itself on all aspects of the situation so that the audience could see the action the planning group wanted it to see, with no risk of surprises. In this situation, even with such briefing a surprise did creep in. In the last few minutes of the role-played meeting, Glover–the man who owned the athletic goods store and who was pushing for the arena–rose and said he could see why the arena was not a good idea at this time. The point is made here to show how such a surprise can ruin the whole purpose. The group spent fifteen minutes in the discussion arguing that Glover would never have done that in real life and, in addition to wasting fifteen minutes, part of the illusion was lost and the learning was impeded. In such cases we want no unforeseen events; hence everyone is briefed about all aspects of the situation and everyone else's role as well.

However, the opposite is true in the following illustration. Here the purpose is to develop sensitivity to hidden clues and to find the key that unlocks the door to progress.

The meeting we envisage is that of a professional association. The members are meeting to discuss "Group Insurance Plans" and have asked an insurance representative to present a plan to them. We select our representative and send him out of the room with a briefing slip. He must have enough information to discuss insurance intelligently, and to know something about the setup and problems of the prospects he is to address. This is not difficult to construct. When he leaves the room to study his information the rest of the group is briefed orally as follows:

> You are salaried persons who belong to a professional association. Supervisors and executive personnel belong to the organization also and consequently you do not want to disclose all your motives in an open discussion. The point that bothers you in Group Insurance is whether it is transferable, that is, if you leave your present post and if you go to another city to work will you lose the benefits. You will not ask this question because you do not want anyone to get the idea that you are thinking of making a change. You will, therefore, be resistant to Group Insurance until the insurance man makes the point. Until then you will be playing "Hot and Cold."

Here you see the idea is to withhold from one the information given to others.

In other instances you may wish to brief the entire group and use a completely spontaneous role-playing plan in which there are no instructions or briefing to individuals. In some cases you might do no briefing other than to ask the group to brief itself. You can see this developed in the following illustration, in which the Camping Association is holding its annual conference. The subject of the session is "Staff Meetings," and the leader of the session starts off perhaps in this way:

In order to discuss staff meetings let's have one. Every camp and camp director runs staff meetings differently and hence any discussion of this will create some confusion unless we have a model with which to begin. May I have some volunteers for a staff meeting? I want three counselors, a specialist, a unit head, a director, and a board volunteer. I mean that is really what you are. (Hands are raised.) Good! Now you folks go into the next room and plan a staff meeting for us with, say, two typical agenda items. When you come back to play it, take on roles other than your real ones; that is, change places with someone else. You have twenty minutes—please, no more. (They go, and the leader turns to the rest of the group.)

While they are out let us establish some criteria for evaluating this meeting. I suggest we break into eight discussion groups as your chairs are so arranged already. In this twenty minutes you work on criteria for a good staff meeting. I shall circulate from our role players to the discussion groups to see what is going on and be of help if I can. Are we all clear on our job?

For a somewhat different type of experience, here is one where both groups are briefed as to the situation but still are left in the dark as to the real training purpose of the role-playing exercise.

To everyone, verbally: This morning we should

like to examine another aspect of problem solving. Each of the discussion groups that have been arranged by the way in which your chairs are placed will send two persons up front for briefing. They will return to the groups later after they have their role instructions. Now will each discussion group begin to work on the following problem. (Pose a problem that is known to be of interest to your group.)

You will now divide the late comers, for these people will be late comers to their groups, into two sections, one from each group in a section.

To the first section, privately: You are highly regarded persons in the community. Not long ago each of you was an important officer in the club. Go into the meeting of your group ten minutes after it has started, listen for a while and when you hear what is being decided, whatever it is, you will not be in favor. Act as you think someone in your role would act.

To the second section, privately: You are new members. You have no position or status in the group or the community. Go into the meeting fifteen minutes late and listen to what is going on. Whatever it is it will not appeal to you. Act as you think someone in your role would act.

Here the group is working on a problem. The effect of late comers on a meeting and the effect of their different status will evolve from the very skimpy briefing given to the groups.

Briefing, then, is to put the audience and the actors into the situation but with only as much as they need to know to accomplish the purpose. Try to avoid introducing red herrings or false trails and irrelevant material. Review your instructions very carefully to make absolutely certain that no necessary facts or instructions are missing, to avoid confusion, misfire, or failure. At the same time keep it down to a minimum to allow for maximum spontaneity. Aim for reality as your model and make sure that the briefing fits your design and is based upon your purpose.

Warm-Up

The warm-up process is one of the most important steps in role playing and yet one that is often neglected. The actor is about to enact a role; he is going to be someone else. The briefing will, at best, give him a very sketchy picture of this person in most instances. Whether he knows the character he is portraying or not he does not know, generally, the relevant or pertinent facts. He needs a framework of agreed-upon background to guide him in being the character. How he will respond and interact with the other actors depends in part upon the background of information from which he can draw. If he has a picture of the role he can be consistent, remain in character, and not be left speechless when an unexpected comment is made.

Whether the warm-up is done publicly or privately depends, as in briefing, on how much you want the others, including the audience, to know. Some may be asked to leave the room while others are warmed up. The warm-up puts the actor into character and fixes in his mind and in the minds of the audience who and what he is in the story. The warm-up consists of helping him to create the character by asking a series of questions to which he responds "ad lib" to make the character his creation and thereby to insure a more natural scene, to make him comfortable with it, and to foster spontaneity. A question-and-answer session between leader, L, and actor, Mr. Hall, will illustrate what is meant:

L: Mr. Hall, you are the administrator of this hospital?

H: Yes, that is correct.

L: How long have you been administrator?

H: Going on six years. (*This is his own idea.*)

L: I see. You are a doctor?

H: No, I'm not a doctor but I am trained as a hospital administrator. (*The latter part is his own idea.*)

L: Does not being a doctor in any way make your job difficult?

H: No, not my job. It does make a difference to some of the medical staff. A few doctors are sticky about this.

L: How does it make you feel?

H: Oh, I don't mind–although I think those doctors are stuffed shirts. In a way I wish I were a doctor. I'd feel more secure. Mind you, I know my job and I run a good hospital–but I would feel easier.

L: I see. What is your biggest problem in running this hospital?

H: Budget. We never have enough money to do what has to be done. We need repairs, equipment, better salaries, more space, and heaven knows what else.

L: Do you mind if I ask your salary?

H: Not at all. I get $8,000.

L: Were you born here in this city?

H: Yes, I was–local boy makes good, you might say.

L: Does this make for any problems?

. . . And so on. Obviously you ask questions that you think will help develop some background and will be useful in the play. The warm-up is not just a chat. It is carefully thought out to supplement the briefing, to put the actor into his role, and to help the audience see the character more clearly. It should be short and be well paced, that is, not allowed to drag.

Take this warm-up used to develop the social or status structure of the organization as an illustration.

L: Miss Warren, what is your work in this organization?

W: I am the paid, part-time executive secretary of the Jonesville Tuberculosis Association.

L: Have you been in that position long?

W: Eighteen months.

L: What does the executive secretary do?

W: She handles the office and routines, runs an educational program, runs the Seal Campaign, and sets up committees and does public relations.

L: To do this, with whom do you work closely? (*Work question*)

W: Well, let me see—the medical officer, the superintendent of the hospital, my own board, doctors, school people, the State TB Society.

L: Who makes decisions that affect your work? (*Authority question*)

W: Everyone—just everyone.

L: Who shares necessary information with you, and with whom do you share information?

W: If I understand you correctly—Mr. Patrick from the State TB Society tells me, Miss Barrow on the National Seals Committee tells me about seals. I must report to the State, the National, the MOH, my board chairman—I guess everyone.

L: To whom do you communicate most closely—you know—about problems, feelings, and things that get you down? (*Informal communication—friendship*)

W: Jean Dobbin. She's my best friend in town.

L: Is she in TB work?

W: Oh, no.

L: Who in TB work?

W: Sometimes Mr. Patrick, but I'm afraid to tell him too much.

L: Who can fire you, or promote you? (*Power question*)

W: My board, but Mr. Patrick evaluates my work, and almost anyone can complain to the board about me. I must keep my figures for Chest X-rays up and my statistics on active TB cases going down.

L: Who gets the credit or the reward because of their position? (*Privilege question*)

W: Well, really! I try to give the credit to my volunteers and board people. This is not a job where people get much credit.

L: Who is the most important person in this Association—that is, who is most valued or has highest status? (*Personal status question*)

W: That depends. Dr. Heartright, our national president, is the spokesman and top man. But I'd say my board president.

If, in this warm-up, the same questions were used with each of the players in the scene you would really know who was who in the association. It would be easy to outline a scheme for determining how people are related to one another in the association; you would collect data for a study, make hunches concerning how these people would act in a problem-solving situation, and—through role playing—test your hunches and demonstrate the problems of this association. Try these questions on a similar problem:

What decisions do you make?
Do you have a free hand?
Where do you get your rewards?
What prevents you from doing a better job?
Does anyone have special privilege?
Who throws his weight around?
Do you have a budget?
Do you sit on a planning or decision-making committee with others?

We do not use warm-up for every role-playing situation. In some there is no need for special role differentiation or for such background as we have shown here. When to have warm-up depends upon need and purpose. For example, in the illustration given later about the office girls and the typewriter (page 157), all that was needed was the information in the briefing. Background material would not have been useful. All that was required was given.

Where the group has some experience with role playing and the actors have no hidden motives they can warm each other up out of the room. By asking each other questions to establish roles and to clarify who is who, the actors learn who each other is and what to expect. All this adds up to building the situation to approximate reality for everyone. Here is another idea. The role playing in this instance will be done by several groups simultaneously; let us say four groups, so that more actors may participate and the audience can break itself down into smaller discussion groups. Let us assume three roles in each group: chairman, church leader, community leader. The four chairmen will meet to map out and to discuss method. The four church leaders will meet to review the situation and why they feel as they do, and the four community leaders will meet to determine their position on the issue. In this way they will warm themselves up.

Every once in a while, with all the best preparation and warm-up, an actor will "pull a fast one" by introducing a piece of information into the scene that no one knew or anticipated. Do not let this bother you. It is part of reality and how the others handle it is useful generally. As groups learn how to use role playing the members are less likely to rely on such "rabbits drawn from a hat" to solve their immediate role problem.

For you who wish to venture, and learn how to use role playing, after your session ask your group to help you evaluate what you have done. Was your briefing clear? Was there enough? Too much? Did the warm-up help? Questions such as these can be asked, and your group, plus experience, will help you to improve your own skill and to learn to use role playing effectively. Evaluation is an indispensable part of this method but it is also indispensable in relation to your whole organization and your meetings. Investigate evaluation. (See *Adult Leadership Magazine*,[1] April 1953, and the discussion of evaluation at the end of Chapter 5.)

There is another form of warm-up that you may find useful. Try it yourself and evaluate its effectiveness or usefulness. It is best used as a stimulator with a new group or a conference, or where you have not done much of this type of program before. A short case or incident or problem story is distributed in mimeographed form. The audience is invited to read it and think about it—but not talk to one's neighbors. When enough heads pop up indicating that most have read it and given it some thought, ask them to put it away. It was a setting-up exercise, and you are now ready to proceed to your first human relations problem in group life.

What kind of case? Something like this, perhaps, if you are thinking of an organization meeting:

> Susan T. had been a member of the Centertown Women's Club since coming to this small city six years ago. She is a schoolteacher. She attended

[1] *Adult Leadership Magazine*, Adult Education Association, 743 N. Wabash Ave., Chicago 11, Ill.

monthly meetings regularly but seldom accepted any responsibility in the Club. Occasionally she would serve on a committee but she would never accept the chairmanship. She said she was too busy.

Jane R. had introduced Susan T. to the Club. Jane R. was a teacher also, but because of evening classes and an invalid mother she missed many meetings and depended upon Susan T. to keep her informed about what was going on in the Club.

Jane R. had arranged to have lunch with Susan T. the day following the November meeting. Susan's first words in reply to a question about the meeting were that she was not pleased with several of the decisions that had been made. For one thing, Susan did not agree with the way the Bursary Committee had been set up. This committee had provided assistance for several girls at high school who came from rural areas and without help could not have continued school. It not only had been a means of helping several girls each year but gave the Club excellent publicity. Margaret G., a public health nurse, had been named chairman at the meeting. Jane R. said she guessed that all the teachers who were members of the Club had had a turn at chairing the Bursary Committee. Susan T. said she thought it should always be a teacher. Jane R. asked if there were teachers on the committee. Susan T. said she had been asked to act but did not think she could accept.

Two other teachers, who were not members of the Club, joined the lunch table at this point; and Susan T. continued to complain about a non-teaching person chairing the Bursary Committee.

Jane R. asked about plans for the Club annual party. Susan T. said that it would be on the 18th this year and that the president had invited the Club to use her home. Susan T. said it was so far out she did not see why they didn't use the hotel. Jane R. remarked that in a home the atmosphere was so much nicer. She asked who was running it this year. Susan T. said the president had a hard time getting a committee named. She had been asked to chair it but had declined. Susan T. said she couldn't take on a responsibility so close to her holidays.

Jane R. asked about the program and wondered what kind of a job the panel had done on the special "National Night." Susan T. said that the program was too long. She added that she had been on the original committee which had planned the program. She had been asked to act because she had attended the National Convention. Susan T. continued to criticize the program and said had she been at the last meeting of the program committee she would have made some suggestions about the organization. She said the whole thing had been planned by three members.

> Jane R. replied that she felt sorry for the program chairman because it was so difficult to find people to take part in the meetings.

By reading the case the group members may be stimulated to think about organizational problems and member behavior. This is a form of warm-up for the session to follow.

We have considered aspects of preparation for role playing. We are now ready to go into the role playing itself.

CHAPTER 4

The Setting and Action of the Role Play

To begin this chapter we shall consider the training design because it provides the form that the play will take, the number of scenes, and the sequences of events.

Considering the Training Design

Let us look at the training design, that is, how the situation will be used in the role playing in order to effect certain results.

The usual type of design calls for the enactment of the role playing followed by discussion. This is the simplest design. As you acquire more skill in using the method you may wish to advance to other interesting variations and combinations.

One variation is to show contrast or comparison between two solutions of a human relations problem by enacting good and bad, or before and after versions. The actors may show the less adequate way of handling a situation and then a preferable method. In some instances it might be unwise to put such value judgments on the solution and it might be more useful merely to show different ways of handling the same problem and invite the group to discuss the advantages and applicability of each.

Where different methods of handling a problem are to be seen and discussed the leader might invite members of the group to demonstrate their suggested methods. This might be in response to the question, for example, "How would you deal with this situation? Come up and show us." Another variation that is very usable is the retake. In this design the actors do the scene and the group discusses it. The actors are asked then to redo the scene based upon the insights gained from the first rendition and the discussion. Still another variation is to ask different teams to enact alternate solutions for a problem story.

Designing the method gives wide scope for imagination and creativity. The possibilities are limitless. An interesting design is that of reversing roles. This is particularly applicable to a two-person play for development of insight into each other's positions. It can be used with retake as well; that is, Alice plays the mother and Jean the adolescent daughter—then they reverse roles with Alice playing the daughter and Jean experiencing her mother's problem of coping with an adolescent. There is discussion, and they redo it with Jean as the daughter again.

There are a few examples of advanced designs which involve more people in the problem solving and thereby provide greater scope for skills practice. One provides for the use of understudies. Here several people understudy various roles and at given times they go into the scene and substitute for the original actors to see what they can do in the situation. In this approach it seems preferable for the substitutes to slip in in much the same way as is done in ice hockey—that is, to interrupt the action as little as possible and pick up where the former actor leaves off. A variation of this plan is to use consultants. In this design the skills role player is given consultants who watch the scene and at his request advise him as to what he should do. When the player wants consultation the scene is stopped while he confers with the consultants privately and then returns to carry on. A variation of this is to stop the scene and ask the audience as a whole, or in buzz groups, for suggestions as to what he should do. Another is to group the understudies into a pool for consultation for each other. In this design the actor requests consultation. The understudies suggest a new plan of action; and a new actor, one of the understudy group, goes in to try to execute the plan. This is a little like a football substitution to effect a change of strategy.

Human relations training and especially leadership training contain many elements of understanding human behavior. The person in a leadership position should strive to understand the people with whom he works. Members, if they are to work together smoothly and successfully, should develop sensitivity to the needs and motivations of their fellows so as to be able to support each other in achieving common goals. There are designs that attempt to provide skills training in sensitivity and human motivation. Here is one. Each actor expresses his feelings periodically through an alter ego. This device is like "Strange Interlude" except that it is another person who speaks the thoughts of the self. The purpose is twofold. The speaker of the thoughts is trying to read the language of behavior and to understand what his partner, the actor, is thinking and feeling, and thereby train himself to be more sensitive to people. At the same time the entire group is seeing how thoughts that are usually unspoken affect the problem solving and the behavior of the actors as they respond and react to one another.

Let us illustrate. A committee is sitting around a table. Behind each member sits his other self. The committee meeting begins. Whenever an "other self" thinks that his real self (the committee member in front of him) is not speaking as he really feels, or that his action is based upon feeling rather than reason, he raises his hand and voices the thought, as for example:

MEMBER: I don't think we would get very far with that suggestion.

OTHER SELF: What is Jones trying to do, promote himself into the chairmanship? I'll have to block that. If I do not I stand to lose status.

One more illustration might suffice for this section, and here we are more concerned with gaining insight into our own ways of behaving. This design is useful to emphasize the importance of a sound approach to our human relations.

Here the purpose of the role playing is to awaken the members to the errors of their ways so that they are ready to learn. Look at this illustration and consider how you might have acted under the same situation in the supervisor's place:

> *Scene One:* Playground in the summer. Julius, aged ten, is in a very bad temper. He gets into a few fights, makes a nuisance of himself and when asked to behave himself he answers the playground supervisor in foul language. He is promptly ejected.

> *Scene Two:* Mr. Playground Supervisor, this has been a bad day for you. You do not feel so well. You have a headache, your throat feels dry, and you are weak. On your way home you decide to go to see your family doctor. For the purpose of this scene I am going to ask you to role-play the doctor, and I will be you. All right–let's go.

In this scene the supervisor will act like a doctor and proceed to examine the leader, ask questions, and try to find out what is wrong–what is causing the trouble. He will diagnose.

When the skit is over the leader might say: "The supervisor here, when he does not feel well, wants an expert to take the time to find out what is wrong. We all do. If we are ill we want a thorough examination and diagnosis; but when Julius is having trouble we do not stop to examine and diagnose–when human relations or behavior break down we just get angry and punish."

The designs described above are suggestions only. There are many variations possible and the successful leader of role playing will fashion his design with the care of an architect, with a functional approach. We would be remiss, however, if we did not examine a somewhat different over-all design called Multiple Role Playing. It is suited to large groups and can be applied to general training sessions.

Multiple Role Playing

Perhaps a description of a multiple role playing conducted recently will make the method clear.

The leader asked that all the chairs be arranged in rows of four with aisles separating the sets of four. When the people came in they were asked *not* to sit with people with whom they came or whom they knew well. When the group of about eighty were seated the leader said:

> I am going to introduce you to multiple role playing invented by a very good friend of mine, Professor Maier.[1] This method has it all over other kinds of role playing because, first of all, everyone is in it and experiences the problem to be solved; second, we do not ask for volunteers to play the roles allowing a few articulate people to benefit—everyone gets a role by chance; third, no one acts up in front of the others—we are too busy playing our role and learning.
>
> Now I am going to give everyone a role sheet with a problem on it. Read it to yourself. Study it—do not discuss it with your neighbors. Figure out what you would do.

Sheets were handed out in this case in sets; that is, every other person got a different story. Here is an example of this warm-up exercise.

---

[1] Norman J. Maier.

You are a member of a Parent-Teacher Association. You and several other parents discussed the problem of children outgrowing skates and the expense involved. A plan was worked out to establish a skate exchange. When it was presented to the Association it met with enthusiastic and immediate approval, and you were appointed to chair a committee to work out details.

The committee decided to invite all children whose skates were in good condition but too small to bring them to the school at which time they would be given a dated receipt. At a specified date all who had brought skates could return to pick a pair that would suit them, if there were any, and take the skates at 50 cents for the service. At the end of a week all or anyone else could come in to select from what was left at 50 cents. There was to be no profit on the arrangement for anyone. The entire project was to be manned by the members of your committee.

When the committee reported its plan the Association approved it with thanks to the committee. At first things went very well. Skates were brought in in large quantities, and many children got skates back that fitted and were serviceable. In several weeks, however, the complaints began to roll in from parents whose children contributed skates but could not find substitute ones in return.

You are at the exchange now, and Mr. Johnstone has come in in a fury. He accuses you of making a fancy profit on the deal while he contributed a $15 pair of skates and got nothing in return.

What are you going to say to Mr. Johnstone?

In about five minutes the leader said:

Put these (*the warm-up briefing sheets*) in your pocket. We shall not use them. This was a warm-up to get you thinking and in the mood. Now we will start. I will distribute the first problem. There are four parts. The person on the aisle will get the stack of role sheets. He will take the top one and pass the stack to his neighbor who will take the next one, and so on. Now, all of you who are Gus, please stand.

Starting from the front of the room you are Gus 1, Gus 2, Gus 3, and so on. (*This could have been printed on the role sheets.*) No one is to discuss his role with anyone else. After you have studied your role and think you know it, fold it twice and in the upper end put your role name and number. Slip this into your breast pocket so that the others can see who you are. Ladies, figure this out for yourselves. Pin yours on your dress or fasten it in some other way.

Now, swing your chairs around to make a circle of the fours. As soon as Gus thinks he knows what he will do when he starts the role playing—

> will he please stand? When enough Guses stand we shall be ready to begin.

When more than half the Guses had arisen the leader gave the go-ahead signal, and each group began the problem-solving role playing. What was the problem?

> Gus was the foreman in a shop supervising twenty men. The jobs were piece rate, and some of the men work in teams and are paid on a team piece-rate basis. In one of the teams, John, Bill, and Ron work together. Each does one of the operations for an hour, and then they change so that all perform different operations at different times. The men decided to do this, they like it, and Gus has never given it a thought. Lately, an efficiency expert has been studying conditions and has reported that this team is inefficient, because if each man worked the one operation he was fastest at and did not rotate, there would be a 17 per cent time reduction for the total operation. (The role sheets give the actual times for each operation.) This is equivalent to 80 minutes in an eight-hour day. The foreman has called the meeting to discuss this with the men. In the role sheets Bill is told that he likes No. 2 position but dislikes No. 3; John, that he will absolutely not work No. 3 steadily even though he is fastest on it, and Ron, that he gets bored doing one operation, and besides it's piece work, so what right

has this so-called efficiency expert to interfere? [2] The role playing goes on until most groups have reached an answer to the problem. The leader calls upon the various Guses by number to report on the solution and to tell how each approached the group. He puts the solutions on a blackboard. When Gus has reported, he asks that play group to confirm it, to say whether they are satisfied and to comment.

It is soon apparent that different Guses tackled the problem differently and that there were different solutions. A point was made of this. After about four Guses reported, the leader asked whether the terrible noise in the room had bothered anyone. There was no response. The leader said the noise was horrible, had no one noticed? No one had. What, he wanted to know, did that mean? Someone said everyone was too engrossed to notice the noise. The moral was obvious.

Multiple role playing, then, is a design suited to larger groups where there are advantages in involving everyone in the role playing all at the same time. It seems to work well with groups which are being introduced to role playing for the first time. It provides a stimulating experience to a group preceding discussion.

---

[2] These roles are reported in detail in *Human Relations*, Vol. VI, 1953, by Dr. Maier.

Rehearsals and Cues

In preparing some kinds of role playing some people like to set up a few cues to be sure they get all the action in, forget nothing, and make it run smoothly. This is appropriate only in the case of the social situation role playing, where it is the story that is important, or an analysis of a problem where the enactment is designed to follow a pattern. Written cues of any kind are frowned upon. Such crutches should not be necessary if the situation is understood clearly. There may be an excuse for cues where there are several scenes, or where there are specific points that must be stressed.

Cues for the spontaneous-type role playing are taboo. The freer it is, the better it is. Rehearsals are entirely undesirable and restricting at any time. It must be understood by all that role playing is not a form of dramatics. One never uses scripts and the more rehearsing there is the less likelihood that it will be natural and as it might happen in reality.

Timing

To use role playing in a meeting or training session, or to use any of the modern meeting inventions, the program schedule must be flexible. It is not advisable to try to force role playing and discussion into a rigid time limit. There must be leeway for development, redoing if necessary, and for adequate discussion. The role playing is not an added extra but an integral part of the meeting plan. The timing is, therefore, a function of the purpose of the situation.

Acting

The actors in the story, problem, or social situation enactment should be asked to avoid long speeches and irrelevant material. They should be instructed to keep the pace up, the dialogue fast, and come to the important points quickly. Note, however, where the role playing deals with the problem-solving process, spontaneous behavior, and interaction for human relations experience, no such instructions should be given. You want people to act as they think real people in those roles would act.

Cutting

It is up to you not to let the role-playing scene last too long. Keep your purpose clearly in mind. You can defeat your purpose by letting it go on beyond its usefulness. Cut the action when in your opinion enough has been seen for an analysis of the problem, or for the actors and audience to have gained some insight, or when the skill has been practiced or tested. Cut it when the audience is stimulated and ready for discussion. If it is a problem story to be enacted, cut it when the group has seen enough to be able to finish the story.

Cut the action when an impasse has been reached and nothing more will happen. Cut when the players are merely redoing or resaying the same things. Cut if you think an actor has had as much as he can take of psychological stretching or if tension has risen about as high as is good for anyone at that moment. Cut if you feel that the situation is approaching therapy. Obviously, cut when the situation has reached its natural end.

CHAPTER 5

Involving the Audience

We are interested in role playing as a method in leadership training and group problem solving. Role playing is not a show for entertaining but a device for stimulating and training our groups. How do we affect the audience in order to achieve maximum results?

One of the advantages in the use of role playing is that it is possible to affect the audience as well as the actors. There are several principles to be mentioned here. We know that leadership and human relations training is more effective when the members participate in the program and are involved in the situations that are being studied. We know, also, that interest is maintained when the people are actively involved in what is going on in a meeting, conference, or course.

Simultaneous Learning Devices

There are several learning devices going on in the same role-playing session. Let us look at them more closely. The actors are experiencing the enactment and are getting the feel of it as well as the feelings of it. The audience is experiencing the enactment through dramatic impact. It is possible to increase this emotional reaction by helping the audience to see what is happening, to feel less like an audience and more a part of the experience. People tend to see more if they know for what they are looking, and if their perceptive organs are focused. There are several interesting techniques for this purpose in addition to the general introduction and briefing.

a. Listening Sections

For this method sections of the audience are asked to listen specifically for certain things such as assumptions, assessments, prejudices, preconceptions, hidden motives, voice changes, tempo, and the like. By concentrating attention people are helped to focus, the effort holds interest, and it produces more points for the discussion that will follow the role playing.

b. Watching Sections

In the same way as above, sections of the audience are asked to watch for body tension, facial expression, behavior change, gestures, and so on. Some may be asked to watch any one role player especially.

c. Explaining

Explaining to everyone what to look for, that is, asking everyone to look and listen for the things listed under (a) and (b) or, as in the illustration of leadership (page 24) asking the group to notice when leadership behavior changes.

d. The Audience Consultants

Here the audience is asked to form buzz groups and discuss how a situation could have been handled more effectively. The actors are then advised by a reporter or a buzz group, and the scene is replayed. The more the audience is involved in the role playing the more and better the participation, discussion, and the learning to follow.

e. Empathizers or Identifiers

Here certain people or sections receive the same role briefing as the actors but instead of taking the actual role they observe it and try to put themselves into the shoes of the particular actor as much as possible. They may be called upon later in the discussion to describe their reactions and feelings.

Analysis and Discussion

It has been said that people never learn so well as when they have had the experience of discussing freely. It is after the role playing in the analysis and discussion of what took place, that much of the meaningful learnings are achieved.

This book is not about discussion methods, and we shall not let ourselves be drawn into a description of discussion techniques. There are some excellent books on the subject to which the reader may refer:

> Thomas Fansler, *Teaching Adults by Discussion* (New York: New York University Press, 1938)
>
> Franklyn Haiman, *Group Leadership and Democratic Action* (Boston: Houghton Mifflin, 1951)
>
> Nathaniel Cantor, *Learning Through Discussion* (Human Relations for Industry, Buffalo 2, New York)

In talking about role playing, one must say a few words about the discussion following the play, however.

At the onset, the leader may ask some very general questions about the enactment in order to set the stage for the discussion to follow. The most obvious but none the less necessary comment, is that the discussion should be guided around the purpose of the meeting so that the group will be helped to perceive the points in the play. This does not mean that he is to tell them *what* they saw, *what* they learned, or *what* to do. Role playing is to stimulate and not to persuade. The enactment and discussion are not to be viewed as fancy substitutes for a lecture. The learning that we hope to bring about comes out of thinking about the situation, the experience, and the resulting insights. It is not the leader's job to tell the members, but even if you think that it is, in matters of human relations, people learn by experience and analysis and not by being told how to act. No one can change another person. It is only one's self that can change one's self.

At the same time, if the discussion is to have meaning and positive results, it must be guided. The discussion leader asks searching questions, opens areas for discussion, asks for the testing of hunches and guesses, and seeks for principles which he may restate to the group.

Do you recall the director in the multiple role-playing illustration on page 101? He illustrated these points nicely.

> *Director:* By the way, did the terrible noise bother you? . . . The noise was horrible. I never heard such a din. Did no one notice? . . . Well, well—

no one. There is a principle here. What does this mean?

Someone: It means, I think, that we were so engrossed in what we were doing that we didn't notice.

Director: Yes, you were so engrossed you didn't notice the noise. Were you interested in the problem?

Many Voices: Yes.

Director: You were interested in the problem and you didn't notice the noise.

Let us look more specifically at the discussion. Here are several alternatives growing out of the design and audience involvement. When the enactment is finished it is preferable to ask the actors to comment on their own behavior after a few moments have elapsed in which people can collect their thoughts. This gives the actors a chance to express their own feelings about it. It frees the audience to be critical. I believe that it is wise to discourage criticism of the acting or role-playing involvement. After all, this is not a little theater group and we are not here to discuss acting. We may ask whether it was true to life and in character. It is better to discuss what was rather than what might have been, at the beginning. What might have been can gradually develop from insights about what did happen as the discussion progresses.

In the discussion we should keep to the problem and the purpose, and not be led off into other things. The leader should, therefore, guide the group to an analysis of the human relations aspects of the role playing. In the discussion the role names should be used in preference to real names to continue the illusion and free the group to criticize the character and not the member. We might then ask the entire group for reactions, that is, what they observed; if it were a skills session, what did the person do or say that helped, that did not help? What principles were illustrated? What reaction or result was observed from this or that statement? Was it what was said or how it was said? What suggestions would people like to make about alternative methods of handling the situation? Why did the actor react as he did? During this type of stimulation there might be time allowed to explore each question with much cross discussion in response to the answers.

We are not envisaging the leader-centered type of discussion here. What do we mean by that? In the leader-centered type of discussion the leader asks the questions and is answered directly. The interaction is always between the individuals and the leader. In this type of discussion everyone talks to the Chair rather than to each other. In fact, it is not a discussion at all but a series of dialogues involving the leader. True discussion permits the filtering of ideas through the minds of others, a give-and-take of attitudes, and sharing. Therefore we are suggesting that the leader encourage cross discussion and withdraw himself from the actual giving of information and ideas. Once he has stimulated the group with a pertinent question he should allow free discussion, by saying little himself until it becomes appropriate to ask another question, make an observation, or restate a principle that has come from the floor.

Periodically the leader may draw in the actors, watchers, listeners, or empathizers for a direct contribution. "Mrs. J, how did you feel when Unger said that?" "Charles, why did you say what you did at that point?" "Jackson, if Charles had been more conciliatory how might you have reacted?"; or, to the audience, "Did you watchers notice anything at this stage of the discussion? How was Charles reacting?" "What light can the empathizers throw on that point?" With each answer and observation the audience is invited to discuss and comment freely.

In the paragraphs above it seems as though the leader is the center of the discussion, but may I emphasize that he is to stimulate, channel, and encourage all the points that are important in the context, allowing the group to do the discussing and the learning. It seems preferable for him to ask others to state the principles, to summarize, and to evaluate different approaches to the problem. Essentially he is most useful when giving procedural help but allowing maximum freedom to the group. His main tool is the question. Do you recall the illustration on page 71 of getting the traditional chairman to give up parliamentary procedure and try a few new ideas? Note the type of questions that might have been asked, not at one time or at the beginning, to be sure. The leader might use them as the discussion evolves or as he thinks they will help the group.

a. How could Jones have acted so that it would not seem like a personal attack on the chairman?
b. What was going on as far as the different committee members were concerned? Why were they apathetic? How might they have been involved more?
c. Would you want to alter the whole traditional structure radically all at once?
d. How would you time your suggestions? What clues did you get that there was any readiness on the part of the chairman to accept any change?
e. Did anyone try to relate new ways of doing things to the chairman's past experience? How might this have been done?

f. Did anyone openly give kudos to the chairman? How was his status protected? How did he react to the suggestions?

It should be reasonably clear by now that the questions evolve from the purpose of the role playing; that the group should be encouraged and permitted to explore the situation freely; that the leader helps focus the discussion through questions relevant to the purpose; that he discourages a leader-centered discussion; that the group solves its problems with procedural help but that the leader does not solve the problem by giving answers.

There are variations to the general methods described above. As a special method, for example, he could involve the group directly in a novel manner by holding discussions with small groups of the audience. When the role playing is finished he comes down in front of the audience and says, "Let us have some discussion on this. The people in this section between the aisles, these four rows. How could Jones have acted so that it would not seem like a personal attack on the chairman?" They discuss for a while, and he moves to another section where he asks another question. This is a method to involve more people.

Another approach is to divide the audience up into buzz groups and ask them to discuss what they have seen, giving them the questions as a guide, or not, or giving each buzz group a different question.

Still another possibility is to ask special observers who were chosen in advance to come up and have a panel discussion about the role play with some able person acting as the panel chairman, with or without the questions. Or, after the buzz groups, bring a member of each buzz group up for a panel discussion. The panel chairman must be good and be well briefed for this to succeed. After the panel the discussion may be opened to the entire group.

A new and different use of role playing involving the audience and stimulating discussion is an application of the incident method of problem solving. In this method the role players enact one incident, a snatch of a situation that might last for a minute or two. They do not enact enough of it for the group to get the whole story.

When the role playing is completed the group is invited to ask questions in order to find out what more the members want to know in order to understand the problem. The role players answer the questions asked, but tell no more than is asked for, as would be the case in playing "20 Questions." When the role players or the group think enough has been revealed for the problem to be clear someone is asked to summarize the facts.

Now everyone is asked individually to write

briefly what he thinks the real problem is, and second, a suggested solution. When this has been done the floor is opened for discussion.

The purposes here are to exercise the group in asking the right questions of themselves in order to diagnose human relations situations, to allow each person to do his own thinking, and to ready the group for a searching and provocative discussion. In this approach the audience is actively involved in the entire process.

If possible no meeting should end on negative learning. The positive elements should be stressed and if necessary the role playing redone on the basis of what the group perceives the better way to be.

Before we close we should make explicit that role playing gives a sample of behavior and we cannot say that what we have seen is the way the members themselves act. We should thank our role players for their help and fine performances, pointing out to everyone that acting out before a group is not easy and the presence of everyone does tend to change the way we might do it under other circumstances; and pointing out to our actors that they, by being part of the role playing, got the most out of the experience. We make sure at the close of any meeting that people feel that something has been accomplished and that they leave with a sense of satisfaction. We make sure that there is some kind of package, neatly tied, for people to take home with them—that is, what did they do, and why! The leader may sum up the main points that came out of the role playing and from the comments that followed.

How do we know whether the involvement of the audience in role playing and in succeeding discussion produces any positive results? Role playing has been subjected to scientific investigation by Dr. Pearl Rosenberg of the Social Relations Department of Harvard University. Dr. Rosenberg used three standard role-playing situations to test the amount and kind of learning induced by role playing. She was interested in learning how it affected the role players, the persons asked to identify with a role but not asked to enact it, and members of the group who merely watched what was going on. During the research project each participant was in each of the above-mentioned situations. You can find a full description of the results in her Ph.D. thesis.[1] For our purposes here are a few of Dr. Rosenberg's findings.

The actual role players focused their observations more upon feelings than upon the content of the situation. They had little ability to suggest al-

[1] *Experimental Analysis of Psychodrama:* Pearl Rosenberg, Harvard University, June, 1952.

ternate ways of handling the situations in regard to their own role.

They had strong emotional reactions about the interpersonal interactions. They were the most productive and active in the discussion following the role playing and *they showed the greatest behavioral change that might be attributed to the role playing.*

The empathizers, you recall, received the same briefing but though they were asked to put themselves into the shoes of the actor they did not enact the role. These people seemed to see more of what went on than the actors. They tended to be very critical of the behavior of the role players and it was they who were the most productive in suggesting alternate ways of handling the situation. There is evidence that they were less likely to change behavior from empathizing alone but *there is greater diagnostic insight into ways of behaving differently.*

The general audience seemed to fall into two classes. One was the passive watcher and the other the active, objective watcher. The first of these did not focus on any one role and was not so clear or insightful as the empathizer was. His focus was more on the total group. He was not critical generally speaking. He did not suggest alternative ways of behaving and he had little feeling. This person would justify some of the criticisms made about role playing. The leader must find ways of discouraging passive watching and converting these people into active watchers. The active watcher had more perception of what was going on and had more analytical interpretations. He was able to see more alternatives for behaving and to be more evaluative of the role of the actor.[2]

It is upon such experience and research that we have based our case. Your satisfaction will come from your own experience. As you use role playing and evaluate its results you will determine for yourself its usefulness to you.

Evaluation

Methods of evaluating meetings and workshops are not difficult to locate. Samples of postmeeting reaction sheets, the use of "post-mortem" discussion, interviewing selected samples of the group, evaluation panels, and so on are reported elsewhere. Most such evaluations seek to determine how the members liked the meeting but do not evaluate the method or the actual learning involved. How can you find out whether role playing in your meeting was successful? It is very important that we do at-

---

[2] For a very informative analysis see, *Exploration in Human Relations Training* (National Training Laboratory in Group Development, Washington, D.C., 1953).

tempt to find out whether we have developed any new learnings. It can be said that you have not taught if the potential learner has not learned, that the experience has been a waste of time and effort if no change has occurred, and that no matter how sensational the method, it was a failure if the results were negative. In addition, neither you nor the group will be helped to improve the sessions without an evaluation of what has been accomplished.

Although it is beginning to sound like a theme song, the evaluation must depend upon your purpose. You cannot assess success if you did not know what you wanted to achieve in the first place. To evaluate your role playing, then, you must start with a purpose and then try to measure how close you came to achieving the purpose. It is important also to evaluate the process, that is, how you achieved what you did.

There are several suggested ways of approaching an evaluation of role playing and the learning that may result. A likely one is for the group to discuss the role playing. In so doing it can determine how real or meaningful the problem was and how clearly or usefully the situation was established. It would judge whether the situation and roles were realistic. The briefing and warm-up would be assessed and finally the enactment. At this point the group might list the principles or new ideas gleaned from the role play and check them against the objectives.

To facilitate the process described above an observer might be used. Here one person watches the entire procedure and records his reactions against a carefully prepared evaluation schedule. His report to the group is then used for purpose of discussion.

There are obvious values to such a group evaluation discussion, and within the discussion itself learning may be strengthened. However, there are weaknesses. One is that some people may sit back and let the others do the thinking. Another is that group forces to conform may prevent some opinions from being expressed. To offset these dangers it might be preferable to ask the members individually to fill out evaluation forms.

If forms are used they should be both specific and general. In order to test whether the planned material was learned the members might be asked to list the points that were demonstrated in the role playing. Another method is to list the main ideas you hoped would be learned right on the form and ask the members to rate how they thought the points were made under headings such as these:

> Very well done—got over clearly and effectively.
>
> Rather good—but some fairly noticeable limitations. So-so—about average.

Rather poorly—not a complete failure but almost missed.

Very poor—didn't make it at all.

Then, to allow for general reactions, provide space for reasons for the evaluation made and for comments.

The progress of learning is from awareness, to understanding, to doing something based upon the awareness and understanding.

The best evaluation, of course, is a follow-up, to try to determine whether, in fact, people do behave any differently in human relations situations after some training or whether they can act on any of their new learning.

Summary

1. Pick or develop a usual, familiar problem of interest to the group.
2. Enact and demonstrate different ways of dealing with it.
3. Involve the audience by asking sections to watch and listen for differences in behavior and feelings.
4. Cut when the point has been made or the behavior is clear.
5. Discuss.

6. Ask the actors how they felt and how they think they behaved.
7. Discuss.
8. Draw teaching and learning points as they are applicable.
9. Evaluate.

CHAPTER 6

The Leader of Role Playing

Whether the role playing is preplanned or it arises out of the meeting it needs a leader. The leader helps to design the action, direct the procedures, and develop the sequence. He helps the members and audience to become involved. His responsibility in directing is to maintain spontaneity and reality, to help the people derive values from role playing, to protect the players, and to stimulate the discussion so that insight and knowledge ensue. We would conceive of a small well-knit group that is so mature and well trained as a group that every member would share in setting up the role playing. This is not the usual situation. It is more usual for groups initially to resist. Many groups fear and hold out against new methods. The members feel shy about trying to act in front of everyone and there is a tradition of listening to speakers.

To help train in human relations and more specifically in leadership training, the atmosphere should be nonpunitive, warm, easy, accepting, with freedom to discuss, to explore, and to learn. If these factors are not present no amount of method or technique will unearth the real concerns of the group and if you do unearth them the group will hide behind all kinds of dodges, and will fight change. For these and other reasons we must understand that no group can be pushed into selecting problems for study, into wanting to do something about its problems, or into role playing.

Another caution is in order here. Easy technicians come and tease problems out of groups, go through all the "right" motions, list many problems and role-play them, as well as using other new meeting techniques. It looks good. Technique, a bag of tricks, and the personality voted most likely to succeed do not succeed necessarily in the sphere of helping organizations to work more effectively. There is no substitute for sincerity, respect for people and a belief in them, nor for the establishment in the hearts of the group members of a desire to improve their methods and the attitude that your ideas may help them to do so.

Whether you be leader, trainer, or member, if

you intend to direct role playing, begin by knowing yourself better. It is hardly possible to understand other people or to help them understand themselves if we do not understand something about ourselves and our own motivations. Human relations reality practice begins at home, meaning with one's self. If you are in a leadership position why are you a leader and why do you want to be one? What are your own personal needs and will they interfere with your helping others?

If your motives are, in truth, to acquire prestige, to be a very important person, to show how smart you are and to direct—that is, push people around—chances are you will not be very successul at helping your groups. Know yourself first, and train yourself before trying to train others. Neither "personality" nor techniques are most important in conference or group leadership. The combination to be desired is an educated heart and educated head. By this I mean a heart that has as its prime motivation helping the group, and a head that has some knowledge and skill in the art of working with people.

If you are easy to anger, cannot take criticism, blow up if things go wrong, expect fast results and have not the patience to let people move as fast as they will, or do not believe in democratic procedures, go to work on yourself first.

Never force people to want to learn. Encourage, motivate, lead, but do not force. Inside everyone is an automatic response control. When that control turns itself down it cannot be pushed up by anyone. It will not come up until the person himself allows it to come up. When the atmospheric conditions are right the automatic control will rise and respond. It cannot be pushed!

As a person assuming leadership you should support and encourage everyone in the group. If you do not think what they say or how they act is appropriate you may comment, surely—but whatever the statement or action, accept the person in a friendly and sympathetic manner, not patronizingly. And it goes without saying that we do not talk down to any group.

Try to keep the focus where it belongs: on the group. Role playing is a procedural help, a tool. You are not there to solve the problems of the group. It is the group that defines, examines, and solves its own problems while you help it to learn to use this tool to do the job. It is important that you know the wants and needs (in relation to the group's operation) of the people in the group, however, before you can use role playing effectively.

Let us emphasize again the role of the leader, because there is a hopeless amount of confusion around the question. In our town an organization role-played problems followed by discussion and expected the leader to tell the members exactly how the problem should have been solved and how the main characters should have behaved. This is a serious misconception of the use of role playing and discussion. The leader's job is to help the group members understand and solve their own problems. Some people have gone too far the other way and say that the leader must not do much of anything and it is up to the group members to do everything—with emphasis on the group as the teacher, learner, change agent, and general factotum. This is the ultimate ideal—the state of perfection. In most cases it is unrealistic. I have tried to explain this in greater detail in other writings.[1]

The leader is the one who enables the group to learn, but it is the individual members who must learn for themselves. Role playing is not therefore a device for giving the answers. It is not designed to persuade the group or audience to a specific point of view. It is to stimulate and encourage thinking. As a result the design is not the same as a demonstration of "this is how you do it," nor should it be "loaded" to convince the group. The design is based upon reality practice and should allow for growth by permitting the participants to have the

[1] Alan F. Klein, *Society—Democracy—and the Group* (New York: Whiteside, 1953).

opportunity of seeing the situation with new glasses, to see what they may not have seen before, and to experience a change without having to go somewhere else to do it.

CHAPTER 7

How Role Playing May Be Used

We have discussed the reasons for and the techniques of using role playing as a training device. Out of the material let us try to systematize the uses and draw out some general principles. Let us remember that our design must of necessity depend upon the purposes to which we are putting the role playing. The major uses for role playing are these:

1. To stimulate discussion.
2. To train in skills.
3. To train in sensitivity and acquire insight so as to solve social and human relations problems.
4. To deal effectively with certain emotional problems that block group productivity.

We shall examine these purposes in greater detail.

To Stimulate Discussion

It may happen that our group is not stirred up enough about a subject to be stimulated, and hence is slow to discuss; or perhaps it needs to be warmed up. To begin a discussion at the outset of a meeting tends to be difficult. We use speakers to start the ball rolling and hope that a good discussion leader through provocative questions will draw the group out. Maybe the group does not understand the subject well enough to risk discussion, or fails to see the subtle implications. More likely it may not feel the problem. By taking the group right into the situation through role playing every last member may be reached. Everyone has a chance to share in the group feeling in the same way as when one sees a moving play. The live presentation has more realism than even a motion picture. No matter how able a speaker may be he cannot create this illusion of reality. No matter how well a written "case" may be presented for study, it needs people acting it out to make it live for the audience.

Because the enactment lives and transports actors and audience into the situation by virtue of the shared emotional experience everyone is participating whether he speaks or not. The likelihood is that the reaction will prompt more people to speak spontaneously.

Take for example the following simple scene concerning a typical teen-age problem that might be discussed by a parents' group.

FATHER: I told you distinctly to be in by 11:30. Tomorrow is a school day. I cannot have you out on the street at all hours of the night. Here it is midnight and you are just wandering in.

DAUGHTER: But, Dad, it's only a half hour later. We missed the bus.

FATHER: Missed the bus. Every week it's a different excuse. Leave on time and you won't miss the bus. I told you what would happen, didn't I?

DAUGHTER: I'm the only one who has to be in so early. Everyone else can go out for a hamburger after the dance but me. I'm always the baby. They think I'm treated like a child.

FATHER: I don't care about them. I'm not *their* father. No daughter of mine can land in here at midnight on a week night. I won't have it, do you hear?

DAUGHTER: I'm so miserable. I could just leave here and never come back.

FATHER: That may be just what you'll have to do if you keep this up.

DAUGHTER: Are you threatening me?

FATHER: Just for that you can't go to the Prom Dance next week.

MOTHER (*enters hurriedly at that*): But John, what is so terrible about a half hour? She could have missed the bus. She has a new dress and a date, and she can't break it now.

Even if you do not have this problem you cannot resist being stirred when it happens in front of you. Surely you want to tell John that he is getting nowhere fast. Or maybe you identify with the father and think our daughter should be in early on a week night. Whatever you think, of one thing you are certain—neither party is helping to solve the problem, and mother is just making it worse. How would you suggest it be handled? The discussion is on.

Are all meetings concerned with learning? The purpose of our organization is to provide some satisfaction to its members whether or not it be an educational or a training group. When the social club engages in its activities it is interested in the values the member obtains from them, and each member is interested in his own satisfactions and growth. Why do people belong to our organizations? In its simplest form the answer is this: in our society and tempo, pressures, tensions, and struggles are so exhausting that the group (club, family, organization) is the one social institution which protects the individual from personal disintegration. In his group life he grows, he changes, he adjusts to the life struggle. The social life of our community is the safeguard of its stability, and our organizations are the bulwark of that social life.

Adjustments and changes of opinion are important aspects of all meetings. Social learnings are vital to the mental well-being of all people. All life requires growth. People are concerned with improving their methods of problem solving, getting along with each other, learning to work as a group, and dealing with the everyday minutiae of living.

Sometimes we spend an extraordinary amount of time getting the interest and attention of an audience or meeting group. As is to be expected, people come to our meetings with many other interests. Evening meetings come after tiring days, and daytime meetings are competing with other pressures. Because of these distractions ways must be found to arouse interest quickly so that we can get to the business at hand.

People come to a meeting bringing with them all their experiences. Of necessity these experiences differ from person to person. When discussion begins, then, each person is talking from a different background, or frame of reference, and hence communication may be distorted. Role playing provides a common base for the discussion because everyone at the meeting will have shared, seen, and heard the same incident together and can begin discussing it. This may be the only basis for common experience the group has. In addition to its being a common starting point because the people experienced it together, there is a common bond developed, a group feeling, a "we-ness" that helps weld the meeting together; for only we have seen this incident, and hence it is ours to share and discuss. Moreover, because we have seen it together, up in front of us, it is something that is safe to discuss; and we can begin talking with a sense of security.

In some instances the group may be reluctant to express its feelings. This may be because it is not sure of how acceptable the members' feelings are, each member not knowing the reactions of the other, or it may be the ordinary inhibitions of polite society which seem to frown upon a display of feeling. If the meeting is to be successful in the sense that it gets down to the fundamentals and deals with the problems that really interest the members, feelings must come out. If attitudes are to be affected and learning ensue, feelings must be dealt with; or, to put it another way, if feelings stand in the way of learning, they must be released.

Sometimes resistance to any change comes about because of strong feelings that are vague even to the holder of them, and some help must be given if those blocking feelings are to be released. Role playing, by expressing publicly a wide range of feelings, may release a group and, or, individual members, freeing them to deal more objectively with their feelings.

An example may clarify this further. In a child study group, for instance, the group is role-playing:

MOTHER: Look at this report card. All failures. (*To the child*) You will have to do better than this. No bicycle for you unless you pass. You come home every day from school from now on and study *before* you go out to play. (*To her husband*) If you took more interest in his study this might not happen. Instead of watching the hockey game with him why don't you go over his lessons? (*To herself, aloud*) It is really my fault. I am stupid and he has inherited my stupidity. Why do I punish him for my sins? If I gave him the kind of home he should have he would be different. I never should have had children because I don't know how to cope with them. My heavens, John, why don't *you* do something?

Here the role play brings out, into the open, feelings that we rarely admit even to ourselves, but because they have been expressed, members of the group can be freer in identifying with the mother.

Another of our problems today is communication. We do not communicate adequately. Many of our misunderstandings arise because of this. We say what we think we mean, but the hearer may hear every word clearly and interpret what we have said differently than we meant it. We may communicate the idea but not the feelings that make the idea have different connotations. We may tell the story but fail to get across the nuances, subtle shadings, and telltale clues. Role playing tells the whole story. It communicates the picture, as only it can, with more of the undertones and overtones. It is high fidelity communication.

There are times when a group seems to feel that what it is considering or discussing is academic or theoretical. It may have been put on the agenda by a planning committee, or the executive, and the meeting cannot seem to feel that it is important because it is unreal to them. The members may see its importance but still deal with it in an idealized, theoretical way. Role playing makes it seem real because it brings the incident to life, dramatically. In addition, even if the incident is admittedly real, when being discussed from a description only it is seemingly removed as is any verbal account of an incident. The presentation makes it seem real.

Consider for a moment the Women's Auxiliary which is involved in a fund-raising campaign. The canvassers are training themselves for the door-to-door approach; what to say, how to answer questions, how to deal with apathy, skepticism, hostility.

To talk about it is fine but when several role-playing incidents are enacted, with the canvassers actually doing the job, the "how to" seems real and can be discussed through a protected experience.

Our purpose may be to present a problem for study. This idea comes closest to social drama or dramatizing a social situation for study. This is, in a sense, the case or incident method done dramatically. The entire case or incident is presented so that it can be seen, discussed, and analyzed by the group. Here is an example:

> The local librarian has been in that position for eight years. She is respected and has never been accused or suspected of any but the highest morals. A local group climbing on a bandwagon publicizes the fact that some volumes in the library are considerably left of center and makes representation to the library committee to have them removed and burned. The committee orders the librarian to remove all the questionable books and send them to the chairman. This she does.
>
> Some weeks later, however, a member of the local group finds a copy of *A History of the Communist Party in the U.S.A.* on the shelves in the history section. The librarian claims that she missed that one, but the group demands her dismissal.
>
> In the first scene we see Mr. A, a member of the

> library committee, at home discussing this with his wife and a friend. He says that he has faith in the librarian and cannot see this as grounds for such action. His wife reminds him that he plans to run for school board. His friend tells him not to be a fool, the local group is too strong to buck. Mr. A tells them how helpful the librarian has been to him in his work and in preparing his speeches.
>
> In the second scene we see him on the way to a meeting with another library committee member who says that he heard that the librarian at one time belonged to a doubtful organization and we must protect our children and weed these people out of influential positions.
>
> In the third scene the library committee meets and discusses the pros and cons.

Now perhaps we have the entire case before us, and the group discusses civil liberties and what a community does in such a situation. Maybe it wants to interview the librarian, discuss the causes of such a situation, explore the ethics, and so on. The role playing is used here to present a social situation for study and discussion. This is an extremely useful device in analyzing for discussion intangible social situations such as the public relations that our organizations have.

So we see that role playing can be used in several ways to stimulate discussion.

To Train in Skills

It is safe to say that many organizations suffer from a failure of their members to know and understand goals. One can almost always trace poor morale, apathy, and other similar ills in part to this one factor. Some groups try to deal with this by giving the new members copious printed material. This is not too successful, usually. Some approach the problem by telling the members. After five successive years of an annual reading of the purposes of one association, the planning committee of the annual conference decided to act out the points. All at once the platform came alive, not only to the audience but to the committee, for to the officers the exercise of having to role-play what had heretofore been just words was an experience leading to deepening understanding.

The use of role playing in this context is akin to orientation. New committee people can be oriented to their tasks through role playing as can a host of other functioning organizational members. This is especially true here because the way we behave in our group is the role we live in fact. The role everyone lives is the part he or she plays in any specific group to which he belongs. In order to learn a new way of behaving, we must change the role and so now we "play" a new role; we orient ourselves to a new part. After we have "played" it and become oriented, that is, put ourself into the new position, we can then *take* the role if it suits us. By this is meant that we are no longer playing the part but we become the part and function appropriately within the new frame of reference.

There is an inevitable interrelation among these various purposes to which role playing can be put. From what we have said about orientation it is easy to see how role playing can be used profitably to train to do most jobs better. In industry, role playing is being used more and more for job training. One large internationally known company uses it almost exclusively for its sales force training. In our discussion, the jobs for which we train are the jobs in our organizations. The most important job of all would seem to be that of working with other people.

There are obvious jobs in any organization from the officers, chairman, and statutory positions up and down. There are, however, many jobs that escape our notice. In order for any meeting to operate smoothly and efficiently and move toward its goals many such jobs must be performed. Some people call them "roles" but in order to avoid confusion, we are going to refer to them as "functions," specifically member functions. If these functions are not performed properly, and at the time when they are needed, we experience organizational disinterest and frustration. Since this is not a book on organizational life in general, we cannot elaborate and describe the process of group participation, but only illustrate the application of role playing to training ourselves to do our jobs better. There are some fine books available on the jobs themselves.

Some of the jobs for which members should train are these: how to summarize points in a discussion; how to and when to ask for information; how to give information; how to enable others to speak; how to put a point simply and briefly; how to detect vested interest; how to test the validity of an argument; and how to facilitate decision making. Some organizations assign most of these functions to the chairman. Chairman-focused organizations may find, on close examination, that this perpetuates a situation in which the person in the chair is the only one motivated to further the group's goals and he must constantly egg the members on. Where the members assume the necessary jobs, everyone is motivated. They may find, also, that in a chairman-focused meeting it is the chairman that grows and develops rather than the members. They will find a scarcity of leadership, also. In our organizational life today members must train themselves to do their jobs better.

Leadership training is of concern to almost all clubs and groups. This is so because many persons seem reluctant to assume leadership responsibilities and organizations have a dearth of leadership. It is true also, because many do not use what leadership skill they have, or are not aware that they have any. We are not discussing the training of leaders. Perhaps we have too many leaders but too little leadership. For a long time the emphasis has been on selecting and training leaders to the neglect of the members. The emphasis is gradually being directed to training the members in the skills of being members. One skill of membership is the skill of assuming certain leadership functions. What is the point in training the chairman to keep the discussion on the topic? The members are adults who are discussing topics of concern to themselves; might not every member assume the function of keeping the discussion from digressing? This is a leadership function. It is trained most successfully by involvement in discussion where such skills are practiced. By the same token skills of chairmanship can be learned and strengthened through role playing, as can many other leadership roles. Role playing is an indispensable tool in leadership training.

Most of our clubs and organizations today are interested in human relations. Industry and even the armed forces have realized that human relations skills are as important as or in some instances more important than technical or job skills. Human productivity and efficiency seem to be directly related to human satisfactions in relationships. How to help people to work together is crucial to organizational life and how we handle ourselves is the key to our effectiveness. Take, for example, the following incident:

> The president of the local health organization is a doctor. He is busy but very much interested. The organization is planning a series of lectures and film showings on health subjects, and Mrs. Jenkins has been appointed to and has accepted the chairmanship of the committee to promote and publicize the program. She has a good committee but before she meets with it she calls upon the president to ask him to tell her how to do the promotion, to ask him to attend the first committee meeting, and to write a promotion letter. He sincerely believes that these are her jobs and that having delegated the responsibility to her he has no business doing these things. The human relations skill question is, then, how does a president handle himself when a committee chairman tries to push the responsibility back upon him in a dependent fashion.

Is it not obvious that such training in organizational "know how" can be done better by actual skills practice than it can by discussion? The situation can be role-played by various persons and discussed in order to develop the skills necessary to cope with human relations problems. This is reality practice.

In the area of skills, and this is what we have been discussing in this section, learning can become part of one's way of behaving only if it is practiced. One can learn intellectually and know, but in order to learn to do, the muscles and nerve reflexes must be conditioned to act. Because of this the behavior of skills must be worked at and redone. Repetition is a principle of learning. We must do it often enough to become comfortable in doing and to reduce self-consciousness. Unless the skill is practiced we tend to lapse back into the old familiar way of doing. So many of our meetings, conferences, and institutions rely upon telling the group or showing it how without ever giving the opportunity to try, to test, and to practice. So many of our efforts are ineffectual as a consequence. Role playing provides the medium for practicing what has been learned.

In our social, business, and organizational life many tricky or delicate situations arise. Where they do, we do the best we can with them but too often we think of what we might have done or said sometime after the event has transpired. Role playing may give one the opportunity of training in quick thinking, in a safe environment. It helps to develop some useful and sound reflexes in handling difficult situations.

Some of the hardest things to learn are the old sayings that a kind word turneth away wrath, that you can catch more flies with honey than with vinegar, and that it takes two to make a fight. Learning to accept hostility without getting angry or punitive is one of the most important lessons in working with people. A close second is learning how to analyze and thereby deal with conflict. Either or both of these are extremely difficult to learn in a real situation because emotions are aroused and we just react. When "playing for keeps" one wants to save face and it is threatening to see our own mistakes. In role playing we can afford to make mistakes because there are no dire consequences, and we are able to *play* at the role. In such a controlled environment difficult material can be handled and examined as we learn how to act and how to think about conflict.

When the group faces a problem in its own operation it can role-play the possible solutions suggested by the members and test those solutions right in the laboratory of the meeting. Why is it that Jean cannot work with Joe? He is successful as national representative with most chapters but when he and Jean get together there are fireworks. Why, he wants to know, and how can he "handle" her? After we set the stage, that is, after we comment that perhaps it's how does he "handle" himself, we begin.

We may ask him to describe a typical situation and tell us how she acted. Then we may ask someone to play her role. We ask him how he acted and ask someone to play his role. When the enactment has gone far enough we, as a group, seek to diagnose the relationship problem, redoing, and retesting. Finally and hopefully, Joe will try it himself to apply his insights and acquire skills.

Jean, herself, may pose the question and want help.

In this instance we want to know how Jean operates so as to know what her training needs and problems are. We construct a problem situation, or ask her to give us a typical one and let her role-play it. How is this? You go for swimming instruction, and the teacher stands on the side of the pool and asks you to swim a length so that he can see what you know and where you need help. Because you want help you are willing to show yourself. So it is with Jean. If she wants help she may be willing to show herself. She may feel better hiding behind an assumed role but if she does, it will still show much of her skill or lack of it and give the leader some idea of her level and her needs.

Here is a specialized use for role playing but an important one. Anyone who works with a group whose cultural background is different from his own must learn to understand the culture of the group. Persons intending to work in organizations abroad need such training and practice very much. It would repay management to learn the culture of the working group in the plant, and so on. To acquire this knowledge so as to be able to use it, it is necessary to learn how to think in the cultural language. This we do through studying and then role-playing the other cultural roles. The salvation of the world in this atomic age depends upon our understanding of other cultures. Understanding goes beyond intellectual understanding. It calls for empathy, the imaginative projection of one's own consciousness into another human being. This is role playing.

It is said that the unknown is more terrifying than the worst known. Perhaps that is so. The familiar can be less frightening than the anxiety of anticipation. Through role playing we can enact what is coming so as to reduce the anxiety and ready ourselves for reality and in so doing make it easier to deal with the real thing when it does come along.

Group work students go into the field as part of their training. When in field work they lead youth clubs. To anyone who has never done this before it can loom as a threatening experience. In class they discuss some theoretical principles. They talk about why the members come, what they expect, and what feelings they may have. Then they construct how they might act as a consequence of the foregoing. They talk also about how the student feels and as a consequence how he might act. But this is not enough. They are still in the realm of theory, intellectual understanding, and talk. Then they role-play several club meetings as anticipatory rehearsal. When the student finally goes into the field his initial meeting is no longer new and totally unknown to him. He has done this before and knows in part what to expect and how he might handle himself.

A friend tells an amusing personal anecdote about anticipatory rehearsal. His wife had never been on an airplane before and was quite apprehensive. Wanting to get to Britain in the shortest time she had booked air passage and as the departure time approached she became jittery. He convinced her that it would be useful to role-play it and so for a week before flight time they played at it. She would come into the living room and he, as the flight steward, conducted her to a seat, took her hat and coat, adjusted her seat belt, and brought her a magazine. After a few moments he made noises like an airplane and then said they were airborne. After that they retired. When the flight time came she went off and things happened just as had been anticipated. However, the conditioning had been so thorough that as soon as they were in the air she fell asleep and did not awaken until the plane was at Gander, much to her disgust, for she had missed seeing the city from the air.

To Train in Sensitivity and to Acquire Insight

In any human relations situation people are constantly giving out cues as to how they feel, their attitudes, and reactions. More often than not these cues are not spoken. They are hidden in expression, tempo, loudness of speech, nervous gesture, body tenseness, sitting up to the table or slouching back in their chairs, color, speech mannerisms, and so on. If we learned to understand the language of behavior how much more would we understand people. How can role playing be used to develop social sensitivity?

As a training device we role-play numerous situations and then each of us tries to guess what each of the others was thinking, feeling, or trying to convey. We then ask them to reveal their attitudes and thoughts in the roles they were playing and, as a group, discuss the cues. Repeated practice of this sensitizes us to an awareness of cues and an ability to read something about them.

Closely related to but different from the preceding section is a matter of insight. Many of us do not know how we act in certain situations and until we do we cannot be helped to change our methods for better ones. Take the example of speech. Few of us know how we sound or how we speak. The first time we hear ourselves on a tape recorder we may be shocked, sometimes favorably, but more often we hear things we would like to correct. In a very obvious sense we have gained some insight into our behavior and now see room for improvement. Having gained the insight does not mean that we change. Not at all. We must now put our insight into practice. As an illustration examine the following:

> At a recreation conference the group was discussing the functions of the recreation committee, the chairman, and the professional recreation director. It was suggested that they role-play a committee meeting. Parts were selected quickly and a situation chosen for the meeting. At one point the recreation director was asked for an opinion which he gave in a fairly lengthy speech. Having done this he now felt obliged to defend

> his opinion in several succeeding contributions. When the role playing ended the committee members were asked to describe their reactions.
>
> Statements such as these were made:
>
> "I was prepared to support Roy after his first statement, but he overdid it later and I began to wonder."
>
> "I thought Roy was trying to tell me what to think. I resented it."
>
> "If there is anything I dislike it's being pushed."
>
> "I wasn't given a chance to arrive at my own decision."
>
> In the discussion later Roy said, "I have often wondered what committees thought of how I worked with them. I would never have known if it were not for this today. Now I know why I have missed the boat on a couple of occasions."

Well, Roy got some insight but unless he could put that insight into practice, he probably did not learn how to work with a committee any better. To do this he should be involved in subsequent role-playing sessions to practice some new ways of working. All organizations could afford to engage in training in committee work. All new committee members could be helped considerably to become more effective through such experiences.

In this illustration Roy learned to work with a

committee because the committee members told him how they reacted to him. It can be done differently. One of the members may take on Roy's usual way of behaving and act him out in role playing so that he can see himself. He may also gain self-awareness by trying different roles (behaving differently) to see how others change in their reaction to him as he changes toward them.

A large part of our troubles in solving conflicts or problems is that we cannot see the other man's point of view. Were we able to stand in his shoes and see the problem he has, and were he able to see ours, how much faster could we see our solutions! Too often organizations are shot through with conflicting cliques or controversial issues which seem to threaten the very foundations of the group. In these unfortunate situations the goal or purpose of the organization fades out of sight and all energy is drained into conflict. This is so in our private and social lives as well. How can we deal with it?

You will recall that this situation can be met in three interesting ways. In the first, the actual problem is role-played to bring out the facts and feelings and to explore the situation. Then the parties reverse roles and play the other fellow's part. In order to play the opposite role and try to do it properly one must begin to feel and see what the other person is up against. Now it can be redone in the original roles to see if these newly gained insights shed light on solving the problem. In the second, the group puts itself into the role of the other point of view, for example, in discussing the South African situation, several white people play the roles of native Negroes. To understand how it feels to be members of a minority group, one year, two students elected to role-play a minority role at a large meeting. They had an experience that no amount of talking or thinking could duplicate. A third is to role-play the situation and to ask each of the opposing groups to state the point of view of their opponents to the opponents' satisfaction and then to proceed with the role playing.

Another somewhat different adaptation comes from role playing at another level. For example, a group of citizens role-plays a committee trying to solve the local transportation and traffic problem and by so doing begins to appreciate how complex that problem is and that it cannot be solved overnight or by pat answers. Or the local chapter role-plays the national committee trying to solve one of its problems. In this instance perhaps the national committee has made a ruling with which the local chapter does not agree. When the local group digs in to role-play the problem, it may see the national group's dilemma and why other solutions were not feasible under the circumstances. Learning how to see the other person's point of view is a tremendous asset in human relations and problem solving.

Some time ago I was asked to meet with an organization composed of members of a minority group. The meeting was called to discuss what one should do when derogatory statements or discriminatory remarks are made to you or in your presence. I had the feeling that this group had high status and lived in an area in which this was not a situation which the members encountered personally. The discussion was to be intellectually stimulating but was not of real concern. To bring the experience to the group, a discriminatory remark was passed in role playing where the group least expected it, and being caught off guard the members reacted with considerable emotion. As a result the discussion was animated, the meeting went on heatedly to its closing hour, and groups collected in the corridors to continue the discussion. As an unexpected by-product this group got insight into the fact that it was not free from prejudice itself.

Tension is hard to cope with when the situation is real and charged. Role playing can discharge tension because the personal element is removed. In our roles we are different people reacting with different people, and the roles rather than the real personalities stand out. After a role-playing session we can analyze and examine the issues, having discharged some of the tension by acting it out.

The answer that suits one group may not suit another. Such an understanding may prevent us from relying on pat answers, easy answers, or doing what they did in some other city because it is easier to copy than to think. In order to accomplish this understanding, the method is a little different from the others we have discussed. Here we may use the device we called multiple role playing. Now we pose the same problem to a number of small groups at the meeting simultaneously. The problem we choose is possible to solve but there is no obvious answer. When the groups have worked until most have reached a solution we ask for the reports and tabulate them on a blackboard. It is helpful to ask the members of the groups separately if they are satisfied with the decision reached in their own group. Usually we come out with a number of different solutions which satisfy those who made them and can show that there is more than one answer to social problems and that people see problems differently. For illustration, examine the following problem:

> Five girls work in an office as typists. Obviously, their machines are very important to them because of the quality of their work, ease of operation, and satisfaction. We are given these facts.

Miss Jones has been with the firm eighteen years. She has an Underwood that is six years old. It is not noiseless and although in good condition it is not new. She does not do so much typing as the others because of semiadministrative duties.

Mrs. Brown has been with the firm eight years. She has a Royal noiseless which is twelve years old. It does excellent work but it is stiff. She does the typing for top management.

Miss Carver has been with us for four years. She has a noiseless Underwood but she is not fond of noiseless machines, having been used to the standard. However, she admits that it is easy to use. She does more typing than anyone else because of her job and because she is fast. Most of it is routine, copy, and duplication or stencil work.

Mrs. Gull has been with the firm two years. She is an older woman who had to return to work because her husband is invalided. She has a poor machine. It is hard on her and it does not do clean work. She is slow and makes mistakes anyway but she does not complain.

Miss Sweeten has been with us two months. She has a fine Remington Portable which is really too light for office duty but it is a good typewriter. She is on the switchboard and reception and does some typing but this is not her primary responsibility. She has been promised a full-sized typewriter because this one bounces when she types on it and because it is noisy for the place in which it is used.

The office manager announces that a new, noiseless machine with all the latest innovations will be delivered this afternoon and he is leaving it up to the girls to decide who gets it. He might put a time limit on the deliberation.

We divide into groups of five. The roles are assumed and all groups begin to try to allocate the new machine. To whom should it go? There is no right answer. Different groups will reach different solutions and be perfectly satisfied with their own choices.

The exercise demonstrates the fact that in human relations there are many answers and through such an experience people gain insight into the concept that each group can best solve its own problems without being given "pat" answers by anyone because there are no "pat" answers.

In this situation a by-product can be illustrated: namely, it is easier and more satisfactory for a group to agree upon principles or criteria first before it tries to make a specific decision on the facts. Once the principles are established a solution comes quickly.

Sometimes self-complacency and apathy become opiates to the point where no progress is possible without special insights. As a discussion method some leaders put out a statement that is so negative, threatening, or inflammatory that the group is bound to argue or defend the "truth." The same thing may occur when a group is confronted with reality in the form of the unpleasant truth about social conditions or about their own operations. As this book is being written the press is reporting on such a situation in a friendly country. The television network has shown a program on atomic warfare that has drawn a flood of criticism because it was too realistic. This much we can say for it, it has produced a good deal more discussion than anything less shocking has done to date and may well be more effective than a hundred pronouncements.

We can visualize role playing in connection with community problems such as juvenile delinquency, organizational problems such as the effects of poor public relations, staff problems and the like role-played with stark realism to stimulate action.

On some occasions our own problem is extremely delicate to discuss because of the feelings involved. Some people might be threatened or hurt. Even so, the problem is affecting the organization and must be tackled. In this instance we role-play a comparable problem in a different setting. Thus we can be more objective and direct, discuss the principles, and hope that the persons involved will get the lesson. An example may be useful at this point:

> The problem is that we have an energetic president who gets things done but in an officious and autocratic manner. The executive committee is quite concerned. How can the members broach the question without hurting the president whom they like? In this instance members of the committee attended a leadership conference. When they returned to their own club they were to present a report on the conference. This they did by role-playing it. The role playing took the form of a series of incidents depicting an autocratic administrator and the results of such methods. Then they showed a committee meeting under such a leader and finally said, "In the conference we learned that the principles of leadership are these and the results of dominating leadership are such and such."

Where the question of dominating presidents is fairly common, and this is a general complaint, role playing at a national or regional conference may be a useful device. The players should be cautioned not to ape or caricature any real person's mannerisms.

Some organizations have the problem of status or hierarchy. The dictionary defines hierarchy as "a rank or order of holy beings," and this is precisely what is meant here. Such a situation can be approached at a conference by analyzing the status levels in a totally different and safe setting. On many occasions we have used a hospital staff setting by role-playing the staff meeting to demonstrate how the status structure affects the behavior of the members. Such a demonstration may lead to the observation that our structure bears similarity to the hospital setting.

Another interesting approach to the status problem is to role-play a meeting and have a high-status person come in late. In one approach you can tell the person that she has high status, that is, that she is a very important person in the community, and not tell the meeting—then observe how she acts; or you can tell the meeting that she has high status, and not tell her—and see how they act toward her. To provide necessary contrast you can have another late comer also, but this one does not come in at the same time as our high-status person. He is a low-status person and again we may tell him or not depending upon what we want to demonstrate. The difference in results in the four instances is startling but rather than tell you what it is—why not try it yourself?

In the previous section, mention was made of reporting. Who among us has not lamented about reports? That they are long, they are dry—or just that they are. Role-playing the items of what you did, how you did it, and what you accomplished is sure-fire. Annual meetings usually have some elements of problem solving, decisions to be reached, or resolutions. Now the meeting becomes interesting and the messages get across. Role-play in your annual meeting. Do not miss the opportunity of introducing role playing to your members in this positive and enjoyable manner. A few short illustrations might be useful here:

> A local YMCA role-played its year's program at its annual meeting in a novel manner. It set up a trial to determine whether the YMCA had been guilty of conducting a good program and whether it should be sentenced to continue for another year. Members of the audience were drawn up to act as a jury. Members of the staff were witnesses who were called up to the Bar to answer questions about their programs and Y members were called to testify about their activities and their reactions to them. Board members acted as attorneys, judges, clerks, and so on. There was no script. When the jury found the YMCA guilty of conducting a good program it was a spontaneous endorsement by the community, unrehearsed.

> A citizens' association in a midwestern city role-played a community problem at its annual meeting. It called persons up from the audience and briefed them in a very few moments to depict the persons behind desks at social agencies. Another group became the family of a robust youngster seeking adventure. In the space of a few mo-

ments the young lad was in trouble and was hurried through many social agencies. None of the social agencies sought to co-operate or work with the others, and the lad finally ended up in a reform school where the person admitting him said, "If the others had done a co-ordinated job he would never have had to come here."

The assembly was presented with a situation which called for the establishment of a central clearing and co-ordinating agency in town to cope with such situations as had been depicted. A motion came quickly, the discussion was animated, and a needed service was established.

These illustrations actually happened. They were not difficult to do and they proved to be especially effective ways of dealing with what otherwise might have been dull reports at annual meetings.

CHAPTER 8

The Values and Dangers of Role Playing

In the previous chapter we discussed some uses for role playing. The values of this method have been presented throughout the book in various ways and places. Partly as a summary and also to make them explicit, let us look at the values collected together in one list.

What Are Some of the Values?

1. You can put yourself into other people's shoes to see how they feel, to experiment with new ways of behaving, to understand other people and their behavior.
2. You can use case material which is tailored to the needs and interests of the group that is going to use it. You devise your own situations, establish your own roles as you see them. There

is nothing theoretical, academic, or supposititious about it.

3. You can practice in a reality situation and risk making mistakes, thereby learning. The consequences of "playing for keeps" are eliminated.
4. You can eliminate all the risks and still retain all other aspects of a dramatic situation from real life.
5. You can observe and analyze objectively because it is a role that is being played. Through this medium you can see yourself and see your own mistakes, in a protected setting.
6. You can unload your feelings, release your tensions, and strip down to learn, to change, and to solve problems.
7. You can learn by doing.
8. You can get people to say how they actually feel rather than their saying what they think you want to hear. (Feelings motivate behavior even in role playing.)
9. You can explore your own feelings and gain insight.
10. Role playing is a method whereby you can diagnose the problems of the player and learn quickly what his needs are.
11. You can bring human life behavior into the laboratory.

12. In role playing and subsequent discussion, the group teaches and helps itself.
13. Its potential for training for some skills is unequaled.
14. It is almost sure-fire for getting total participation of all members in discussion and involved in the subject at hand.
15. It is a modern method for a modern age.

Now that we have looked at the values let us examine the dangers so that we may learn to avoid them.

Some Dangers to Avoid

There are some dangers in using role playing, some pitfalls which you can avoid if you understand what they are. Some of these have been mentioned in previous pages, some have not. It would be useful to bring them all together so that the danger signs will be clearer to you.

1. It is not useful to cram a meeting with too many techniques. If you are having a speaker and a discussion period, it is not advisable to add role playing.
2. To use role playing you need time. One great weakness of all our meetings and conferences is that we do not allow adequate time for dis-

cussion. It is not advisable to try role playing unless your agenda is flexible.

3. As your group becomes more experienced in role playing it will know how much time is needed and when role playing is appropriate. Until then you will have to help the group with these limitations.
4. Role playing is a method, it is not an end in itself.
5. The group should be concerned with the problem being played.
6. The role play should be at the level of understanding and maturity of the group.
7. It is not advisable to use role playing as a skills practice device or insight-giving process if the person's boss or his subordinate are present! This applies to status positions outside of an employment relationship also. No one wants to appear at a disadvantage before those whom they supervise or for whom they work. Watch the grouping carefully before attempting certain types of role playing.
8. Bad habits, poor attitudes, and poor relationships are not causes of behavior. These are symptoms. You must go deeper and provide insight into the causes of these external factors if your organizational problems are to be solved.
9. Please do not look for miracles. It took a long

time for people to get the way they are, and for your organization to develop as it is. Neither will be changed overnight. The kind of problems we have been discussing take time to solve. To become aware of them is but one step, to understand them may take longer, and to change behavior is harder than to just role-play it. Do not push. People can change only so fast. They must grow into it as a result of experiences, because they want to and have reasons to try.

10. Keep clear of therapy. You are not a psychiatrist. Guide the group away from psychodramatic situations that will result in personal exposures. Try to anticipate and avoid material that is bound to reveal personal and private feelings. You can guard against this by your briefing and by keeping all analysis on the *roles* and off the persons who play them.
11. Keep role playing democratic. In the last analysis, democracy is the foundation of our entire premise—that people can be helped to solve their own problems and can be stimulated to think for themselves. We believe that free men should know the facts, should be critical (not negative) of their environment, methods, and results, and should know how to change them. We believe that through participation and in-

volvement people can develop themselves and their societies to their potential.

12. Resist telling the answers. (As if you knew them, anyway!)
13. Don't set up the role-playing situation so that there is only one answer possible to the problem.
14. If you do not know the group, watch out lest you as leader be used to put someone on the spot. Perhaps if I tell you how I was once caught it will illustrate this. I was asked, "When you cannot serve the persons who come to you, what should you do?" Before I could open my mouth someone said, "There is a good situation to role-play—how about it?" There was no enthusiastic response. The original requester followed up: "You can be the service organization secretary so as to demonstrate how it should be handled." At least I was awake enough to sidestep that one.

"I don't mind being in the role playing but I don't think it is my function to show how it should be done. This group can work that out far better than I, coming from the outside, can. It knows the problem better for one thing. What is the problem? Can you make it clearer for me?"

The protagonist: "Let's say we have a service organization in town to help parents cope with problem children. Mrs. Brown goes to it and the man there doesn't think his service is the place for her problem so he refuses her. How should he turn her down?"

When I looked around I saw real interest.

"Do you want to role-play this?" There was positive and general agreement. We did it, but it was not until later that I learned that the group had gone along to scapegoat one of those present and had used my session to put him on the spot. This was a real situation we were doing, and the real person was present.

Another time a group wished to role-play the presentation of a budget committee. Here the players did a take-off on well-known local people. It was well done but embarrassing. It was *not* role playing.

It is advisable to avoid the actual situation. Role-play something like it but leave a margin to be safe and to save face.

15. A group may want to play a scene that depicts a problem it is facing in its own organization. The difficulty now arises when someone says, "That looks like us. How much of what was

said is really how we feel?" It is hard to know just when to let the group make the switch to its own problem. One should be aware that it may be this one person only who is ready. Certainly it is not up to the leader to push the point home. If the group are ready to look at themselves they will, as a group.

16. Help groups to avoid problems that are not their own and that belong at a different level. Where the local group wants to role-play and solve the problem by changing national policy, that is, to work on a national problem, it may be wise to point out that this is not for them to solve. About the only reason to play it is to help the local group see the national group's problem and that it is not easy to solve.
17. Do not talk too much. Give the group a chance to talk and to think. How often do you ask a question that requires some thought and, if someone does not answer at once, do you begin talking again? Each time you talk you interrupt their thinking. Each time you talk you may be keeping someone else from talking.

Some Answers to Criticisms Made About Role Playing

It has been said that role playing is not useful because, after all, you really are not doing it, you are playing at it; the very fact that it is so, makes it artificial and just an exercise because to learn by doing means doing it under the actual conditions. Let us agree that there is truth in this but, true or not, is there not much to be learned in a simulated situation?

Much scientific testing is done in a laboratory. The conditions in the "lab" are simulated and often are controlled. None can deny that we have learned much in our laboratories. Role playing is our laboratory for human relations. It is a use of scientific methods for tackling social problems.

Some people say that because role playing is playing roles the emotional impact or involvement is absent. It may be lessened somewhat but it is not absent. Certainly role playing involves the persons more than a lecture could, no matter how skillful the lecturer. We have all experienced being drawn right into the plot while seeing a gripping film or play. We know how it feels to identify with the actors or the situation. There is no question that to enact the role requires greater emotional identification. It may not be reality but it is the next best thing.

Some critics say that the players are superficial, guarded, unable to play with depth and understanding. That depends upon the problem and how close people are to it, to the group, and to the individuals themselves. Role playing can be superficial; but, as insight develops—if the problems are real, and as people get used to using the method—depth and understanding develop. Even small children develop surprising insight through role playing.

Some critics say that role playing can arouse guilt in people as they begin to understand their "mistakes." But understanding of ourselves which comes in any way can produce guilt and discomfort. It is for us to handle it as the occasion demands.

They say that role playing is very threatening because it involves self-exposure. This is true. The atmosphere must therefore be nonjudgmental, the leader accepting, the group agreed that there is to be learning and that hence people are not to be criticized but helped, and the "out," after all, is that we are playing roles. It is up to us to include methods of threat reduction. One of our stated group goals might be that of helping the next fellow to achieve what he wants to get out of the experience. Groups can train themselves to take on this responsibility. Incidentally, role playing of this kind should be undertaken always in small groups. Skills training and insight training are not so appropriate to large groups or conferences.

One hears that the players do not play the roles properly; they overact, or do not behave as real persons would in similar circumstances. Whether the playing is close to reality will depend, in a large measure, on how appropriate the situation is, how much reality there is for the actor and the group in the problem, how clear the problem was made in the briefing, and how skillfully the warm-up was done.

Some people say that the actors may not have the experience from which to draw to portray their roles. This can be true. This may be a strength rather than a weakness. The role playing can begin to give the experience as in the case of anticipatory rehearsal. The audience or group in the discussion will probably readjust the sights and point out how it might have been done more realistically. If no one has the necessary experience it was not an appropriate situation. Remembering basic principles of learning there are two that seem to apply here: (1) go to the unknown from the known, the unfamiliar from the familiar, using bridges; (2) start where people are.

The criticisms related above are good to keep in mind but they are not serious. Many of the criticisms stem from the fact that we have all seen poor examples of role playing led by persons who were not skillful or who had not spent enough time in preparation. No tool or method is perfect. The weakness inherent in this method can be overcome and allowed for. Role playing is a remarkably effective tool if used carefully for the purposes for which it is designed.

It is from experience that I have written this book. Your satisfaction will come from your own experience. I have tried to give some help to guide you. These are suggestions only. I have every reason to believe that you will create and invent new uses and methods that will be of value to you and your particular organization.